BRENTWOOD

OUR HERITAGE

BRENTWOOD
OUR HERITAGE

Frances Clamp

First published 2010

The History Press
The Mill, Brimscombe Port
Stroud, Gloucestershire, GL5 2QG
www.thehistorypress.co.uk

British Library Cataloguing in Publication Data.
A catalogue record for this book is available from the British Library.

ISBN 978 0 7524 5348 4

Typesetting and origination by The History Press
Printed in Great Britain

Contents

Acknowledgements

My thanks go to Sylvia Kent, for all her help and support, to David Clamp, for invaluable computer advice, to the staff of Brentwood Library, to David Webb, and all the contributors to this book. Above all, my thanks go to my husband, Roger, for his help and support in so many ways.

Every effort has been made to trace ownership of photographs and to check the facts given in the book. I give my apologies for any unwitting errors or omissions.

Frances Clamp,
June 2010

1

The Beginning

Early Times

Brentwood is a popular commuter town, situated close to the busy M25. However, throughout the centuries of its existence it has always been a town of passage. Today it overlooks the protected green belt, that vital lung dividing the east of England from the London sprawl. It is also a town with a fascinating past, an interesting present and a well-planned future. In the following pages we will consider how the past, present and future come together to make a vibrant and important town.

Roman travellers almost certainly followed the long, straight road that is now known as Brook Street and High Street as they made their way between London and Colchester. However, there is no sign of any Roman settlement in the area dating from that time. In fact, this was probably a tree-covered area that was part of the Essex Great Forest. It is often beside a road that artefacts are found. The most significant to be discovered was a gold ring bearing a chi-rho Christian monogram, unearthed close to Hillside Walk in 1948.

Sandpit Lane now runs through the site of a former Romano-British camp. The site covered around seven acres, but little else is known about the early history of the area.

Brook Street and High Street are still the major arteries into and through the town. Both have changed greatly over the years, but some of the old buildings that tell something of the town's history remain. Marygreen Manor in Brook Street, with its beautiful half-timbered façade, reminds us of former elegance. On the opposite side of the road stands the Golden Fleece, once a stopping place for stagecoaches, but long before that it was the home of the master of the nearby leper colony. Further up the hill towards the town, large houses are a reminder of the time when the East India Co. took over Warley Barracks. These were used for officers, although now many are divided into multiple dwellings.

Domesday Links

What is now the village of South Weald was once far more important than Brentwood. King Harold gave the estate of South Weald in an endowment to a foundation of secular canons at Waltham and this probably included land that would much later be known as Brentwood. This situation still existed at the time when the Domesday Book was compiled, so the future town received no acknowledgement. In fact, it wasn't until 1176 that an outlaw was mentioned in the Pipe Roll of the

Far left: Marygreen Manor. This beautiful house must have been noticed by thousands of travellers over the years.

Left: St Peter's Church, South Weald.

Exchequer as being Reginald de Bosco Arso ('of the burnt wood'). This later became Brentwood. Whether the 'burnt wood' referred to a fire in the forest or charcoal burning is unknown.

Murder

It was a notorious killing that really changed the fortunes of Brentwood and led to the early establishment of the town. In 1170, Thomas à Becket was cruelly murdered in Canterbury Cathedral. Within a few years, pilgrims were making the often dangerous journey to worship at his tomb. The travellers needed places to eat, rest and pray, and inns sprang up along their route. At the crossroads where Brentwood is now located, a hamlet grew up to cater for the pilgrims' needs. This was the start of the town.

In the centuries since those first pilgrims paused in Brentwood, there have always been a large number of inns, cafés and restaurants in the town. This tradition continues today and doubtless will in the future. Now it is not simply traditional English food that is available; many other nationalities offer their specialties to the discerning public and the High Street and surrounds are well known for the variety of culinary delights on offer. Once again travellers come to the town to enjoy the food and drink.

South Weald

As is mentioned above, South Weald was originally more important than Brentwood. It has had a church, St Peter's, since Norman times and the round arch over the west door is surmounted by the typical dog-tooth pattern so popular at that time. There have been many changes over the centuries, especially in the days of the Victorians when enthusiasts embarked on massive alterations. One such reformer was the vicar Charles Belli, who spent large sums of money on buildings in the town, including schools.

South Weald Church was well away from the main pilgrim route passing through the ever-expanding hamlet of Brentwood and it was felt that a chapel was needed to cater for their spiritual needs. Permission was granted for this to be built in 1221 and it was dedicated to St Thomas à Becket, but it remained in the parish of South Weald.

The Chapel in the High Street

Today all that remains of the Chapel of St Thomas à Becket is part of the tower, a small section of the nave and a plan on the ground following the former outline. Yet this small building played a very important part in the history of the town. Although a subsidiary of St Peter's, South Weald, it was important in its own right, serving both pilgrims and the residents who had settled in the area.

It is hard to imagine now that this haven of peace in the busy High Street was once a place of conflict. However, there have been times in its history when its original purpose was completely forgotten.

It was in 1232 that Hubert de Burgh, chief minister of King John and later of Henry III, fell from favour with the king. Hubert decided that the safest thing to do was to leave the court. His nephew, the Bishop of Norwich, had a house in Brentwood and this is where the worried courtier decided to stay overnight. All went well until he heard that Godfrey de Gravecumb, steward of the royal household, was on the way to arrest him, accompanied by 300 soldiers.

Hubert hurried to the chapel to claim sanctuary. He should have been safe as this could last for up to forty days. Yet when the posse arrived, they stormed the chapel and, ignoring Church Law, dragged the unfortunate man out and took him to the Tower of London.

The chapel in the High Street.

Needless to say, outrage followed. The Bishop of London threatened all those involved with excommunication – no small threat in those times. The king relented and agreed to Hubert's return to the chapel in Brentwood, but things had changed. Guards were posted around the building and only a daily allowance of a halfpenny loaf and a measure of ale was permitted. Later, even that small concession was withdrawn and Hubert was forced to leave sanctuary. He was removed once more to imprisonment in the Tower of London. However, the story does have a satisfactory ending. He was finally released and lived in retirement until his death in 1243, but well away from Brentwood and memories of his time spent in the chapel.

Labour Troubles

Today Brentwood is normally a fairly quiet, law-abiding town, but this was not always the case. The Black Death in 1348-49 and 1361 led to a depletion of the labour force throughout the country. Tax collectors were expected to collect the same amount in taxes as before the plague struck and this led to discontent among the remaining workers. According to records, the amount of poll tax collected in Essex between 1377 and 1381 dropped steadily. Sir Thomas Bampton, Commissioner for Essex, was sent to Brentwood in 1381 to set up a court of inquiry, but the angry defaulters ran the commissioner and his escorts out of town and three of the commissioner's clerks were beheaded.

When the Chief Justice of Common Pleas, Sir Robert Belknappe, arrived to punish the offenders he was captured and forced to swear on the Gospels that there would be no further inquiry. He was also made to hand over the names of those who had betrayed the rioters. Those unfortunates were then beheaded by the tax dodgers and their heads, along with those of Thomas Bampton's clerks, were impaled and taken to London. On the way the group, which had now become a mob, joined up with other angry workers from Kent led by Wat Tyler and John Bull.

This was Brentwood's part in the Peasants' Revolt. Richard II made various promises to the rioters, but they were later revoked. However, there is another link in the town with those troubled times. In the centre of the High Street stands an ancient inn, known until very recent times as the White Hart, but now the Sugar Hut Village. Apparently an earlier inn on the site was visited by the Boy King in the aftermath of the troubles and the later inn received its name from the emblem of the king – a white hart.

Feminine Fury

Peace returned to the little chapel for a while but then, in 1577, trouble brewed once more. The heir to the Weald Estates, Wistan Brown, claimed ownership of the chapel and decided that it should be demolished. He stopped paying the chaplain and the pews, the pulpit, the clock and the great bell were all removed. Complaints were made to the Lord Keeper of the Great Seal, but the squire continued with his plan to destroy the chapel. An interesting insight into law and order at that time was that the inhabitants of the hamlet complained that they were forced to travel to South Weald to attend services and during the time they were away, their houses were likely to be robbed or burnt!

The White Hart, now known as Sugar Hut Village.

At this time, thirty militant women took centre stage. They were led by Thomasine Tyler, who had previously been the wife of Thomas Alderton, owner of both the Swan and Bell Inns. The group seized the schoolmaster, Richard Brook, who they had apparently found in the chapel. They removed him then, after beating him, they shut themselves inside the building armed with a variety of weapons. These included pitchforks, bills, two hot spits, three bows, nine arrows, one hatchet, a great hammer, hot water in two kettles, a piked staff and a great sharp stone. These formidable women were determined to put up a fight.

Eventually Thomasine and some of her followers were arrested, although seventeen escaped that fate. The women were finally released on payment of small fines and Wistan Browne was ordered to refrain from pulling down the chapel. Peace returned and the chapel continued to play an important part in the life of the town. It was many years later that the little chapel was eventually pulled down.

Farewell to the Chapel

It was in the days of Queen Victoria that the chapel that had witnessed so many momentous events in the history of the town finally met its end. It was decided that the building was too small to serve the needs of a rapidly growing population. The fabric of the chapel had been neglected and plans were made to erect a new church on the site of a nursery garden lying to the south of the High Street. The church was built in 1835 and the old building became, for a while, a National School. Then it lost even that role and in 1869 it was decided that it should be demolished. This time there were no militant women ready to fight for their place of worship and, after six-and-a-half centuries, the nave and part of the tower were destroyed. In his book *Fireside Talks About Brentwood*, John Larkin (1850-1926), a well-known local benefactor, described the demolition of the chapel as 'an everlasting disgrace to the town'.

Yet this was not the end of the story. In the twentieth and twenty-first centuries the ruins have been shown new respect. Railings were commissioned by Squire Tower of Weald Hall in 1903 to protect the west end of the building and, in 2008, scaffolding appeared as restoration work was carried out on decaying stonework.

The chapel still has a part to play in the life of the town. An open-air altar has been erected at the east end of the old nave and services, often interdenominational ones, are still held there, especially at Easter time when worshippers process in from many churches in the town. The pilgrims' chapel lives on and we can only hope that it continues to do so for many centuries to come.

The Town Grows

Returning to the story of the ever-growing hamlet, an increasing number of pilgrims travelled along the main roads and this led to a growing number of traders coming to cater for their needs. Inns were needed to offer food, drink and safe shelter for the night, and traders and merchants soon realised that here was a ready market for their goods. At least one of the old properties still exists in the High Street, with the three sections now occupied by shops and a restaurant. The building dates from 1425 and was probably originally a single house with two wings. A narrow alley divides two of the shops and there is an ancient bricked-up doorway that once led into the building to the west. This doorway possibly dates back to the fifteenth century. The passage is the beginning of South Street, once called Chapman's Alley. It is worth standing for a few moments at the north end of the passage on a bleak day in winter as it takes little imagination to envisage the scene as it must once have been. Then pass through and look back at the roofs of the old structure – this view helps to confirm the age of the building.

Returning to the High Street, the property to the east of the old Lion and Lamb public house, now Dorothy Perkins, is a small cobblers. Joined to that is a gabled building, until recently occupied by Clinton Cards. In the 1970s this was due for demolition, but as workmen started removing the fascia they discovered an ancient timber structure. Investigation confirmed that it almost certainly dated from the fourteenth or fifteenth centuries. Fortunately, the decision was made to preserve the timbers within the new building, so a very old part of Brentwood has been kept for future generations.

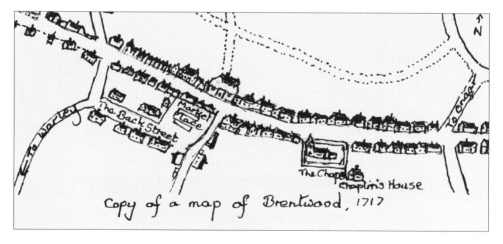

Copy of an early map of Brentwood. (© Frances Clamp)

Above left: The outline of a medieval timber-framed house and shop found during the archaeological dig of 2000 in Hart Street.

Above right: An ancient doorway beside Fentons shop.

Hart Street

Running parallel with the High Street on its south side is Hart Street, formerly known as Back Street. With the High Street, this was the early centre of development in the town. Now a comparatively quiet one-way street, it was once the heart of the medieval trading community. Over the years the old shops at the junction with Kings Road fell into disrepair and a fire hastened the end of these buildings. Plans were made to build apartments but, before construction work started and following demolition, permission was given for an archaeological dig, which took place during 2000.

Some fascinating discoveries were made and the archaeologists stayed for an extended period, discovering more about the medieval Brentwoodians who lived and worked in that area. Some of the finds dated back to the twelfth century. Among other things discovered there was a medieval bread oven, some green glazed pottery originally from London and a sixteenth-century iron foundry hidden below a Victorian cellar. The builders moved in and the old site was covered, although the artefacts have been carefully preserved. Close by in Kings Road, on the corner of Chatham Way, a small garden has been created with the outline of a medieval house and shop laid out on the ground. This replicates the plan of one uncovered during the excavations. Now it is possible for people from the nearby shops and offices to spend their lunch breaks in this peaceful area, perhaps recalling those workers who toiled close to this spot in an earlier age.

Further along Hart Street, to the east, is where it is believed the market was once located. This included the Shambles, where meat was sold. Such areas were well known for their pungent smells as waste meat was often left to rot on the ground beside the stalls. Perhaps this is one aspect of medieval life best not imagined. There is also an old, single-storey building on the left as you go towards Crown Street. This is now used as a tattoo parlour, but the bricks that can still be seen on the sides obviously come from much earlier times.

The shops in Hart Street before there was a fire and demolition. This was the site of medieval buildings. (By kind permission of Sylvia Kent)

Sir Anthony Browne

Anthony Browne is well remembered in the history of Brentwood for two special, but very different, reasons. He was active in the events that led to the death of the local martyr, William Hunter, and he later founded Brentwood School.

Born in Essex, he went to Oxford before starting a career as a lawyer. He became involved in politics and served under three of the five Tudor monarchs: Edward VI, Mary Tudor and Elizabeth I. His links with Brentwood started when he bought Weald Hall and the manors of Calcot and Costed following the Dissolution of the Monasteries. His knighthood was awarded in 1566, but he had little time to enjoy this honour as he died childless the following year. His great-nephew, Wiston Browne, was his heir and it was he who so offended the women of Brentwood when he tried to demolish the chapel.

William Hunter

A blot on the history of Brentwood is the story of William Hunter. As a teenager, he lived during the reign of Mary Tudor but, unlike the Queen, he was a passionate Protestant, a dangerous choice in those troubled times. An apprentice silk weaver in London, his religious convictions led to him being dismissed by his master and he returned home to Brentwood.

Before long he was again in trouble, this time with Thomas Wood, the vicar of South Weald. William vocally denied the Roman Catholic doctrine of transubstantiation and he also felt that everyone had the right to read the Bible in their own language. At that time, English versions of the Bible were being smuggled into the country from the Continent. Anyone who disobeyed the teachings of the Church in the days when Queen Mary ruled the country knew that the penalty was almost certain to be death.

Here the stories of Anthony Browne and William Hunter come together. Browne was the local magistrate who decided to send the teenager to appear before Edmund Bonner, the Bishop of London. The bishop tried, unsuccessfully, to argue with the youngster and then had him put in the stocks for two days. This did no good and although the bishop made every effort to get him to accept Roman Catholic doctrine, he steadfastly refused.

Finally the nineteen-year-old spent a month in Newgate Prison before being returned to his home town for execution by burning at the stake. The year was 1555.

William Hunter spent his last night at the Swan Inn, although not in the building of that name now to be found in the High Street. He was visited by his family before being taken to the archery butts where, in the presence of Anthony Browne and the local townspeople, he met his untimely end.

An elm tree grew close to the spot of the martyrdom and for many years this was preserved in Ingrave Road, outside Brentwood School. At one time the trunk was apparently 26ft in diameter but, by the late nineteenth century, all signs of life had disappeared. By 1952 it was decided that it was no longer safe and what was left of the stump was removed.

This oak tree was planted in 1936 to mark the accession of King George VI and to replace the ancient elm that grew close to the site of the martyrdom of William Hunter.

A memorial to the young martyr was erected by public subscription in 1861 and it still stands close to Wilson's Corner. In 1909 the original Wilson's Store was completely destroyed in a devastating fire and the stone cracked in the heat. It was later repaired, but signs of the damage can still be seen today.

William Hunter's name lives on in the town. William Hunter Way runs parallel with the High Street to the north and that is where the Sainsbury's superstore is situated. In 2009, a major road development scheme led to this becoming an ever busier road and the name of Brentwood's youthful martyr is becoming even better known.

The Petre Family

Also during the time of Henry VIII, another local landowner rose to prominence, benefiting from the Dissolution of the Monasteries. Sir William Petre acquired the manor of Gynge Abbess, formerly in the hands of Barking Abbey. He had the existing building demolished and built Ingatestone Hall. Later he served both Edward VI and Queen Mary.

Only one of William's sons, John, survived him when he died in 1572. He bought West Horndon Hall, originally built in 1414, and spent the following twenty years rebuilding what became Thorndon Hall. John received a knighthood in 1576 and later he became the first Baron Petre.

Leprosy

One of the most dreaded complaints before and during the Middle Ages was leprosy. This disease could affect people of any age or social status. Brentwood had its own leper hospital situated at the bottom of Brook Street, well away from the centre of the growing hamlet. The master of the colony lived a short way from the actual hospital, where the Golden Fleece now stands. In fact, timbers from the master's house can still be seen upstairs in the restaurant where the old and new beams have been carefully blended. The building was at one time used as a coaching inn where fresh horses were available for travellers before the steep climb up the hill to the town. It is now a Harvester restaurant and was once known simply as the Fleece. The original building is believed to date to the late thirteenth century.

A chapel dedicated to St John the Baptist also stood nearby, but this ceased to be used at the time of the Reformation and the land was bought by Sir Anthony Browne and Richard Western in 1553. We are reminded of the old leper hospital in the name Spital Lane, which is to be found close to where the colony once stood.

The Reformation and the Dissolution of the Monasteries

As in many other parts of the country, the Reformation and the Dissolution of the Monasteries led to great changes in Brentwood. Property that had previously been held by the Church quickly passed into the hands of laymen. We have already seen that both the Petre and Browne families benefited from these changes.

The Golden Fleece, former site of the leper colony master's house.

Brentwood Chapel passed into the care of Anthony Browne. The chapel had its own chaplain, who was paid the princely sum of £5 per annum, and the new lord of the manor promised to continue with this payment. However, Anthony's heir, Wistan Browne, decided that such payment was inappropriate and this led to the trouble with Thomasine Tyler and her followers.

Wistan soon thought of another way to obtain money. His great uncle had established Brentwood School, but as the new lord of the manor he decided to seize the property. Again, angry local people took action, petitioning the Lord Keeper of the Great Seal. The hearing went against Wistan and, in 1573, he was forced to restore the land to the school. In 1616, a later Sir Anthony Browne refused to pay the chaplain but he too found that judgement went against him and a chaplain continued to serve the chapel.

Times were changing. The town that had grown up to serve pilgrims was becoming established in its own right, although still under the jurisdiction of South Weald. It was increasing in size and influence and the years to come would see ever more changes to the town and its people.

2

A Town of Passage

As we have already seen, from the very beginning Brentwood has been a town of passage. Although no known settlement existed in the time of the Romans, the road from London to Colchester passed over the ground where one day the town would be grow. As the pilgrims set out on their journey to Canterbury, this was a place where they stopped briefly before continuing on their way. Developing on an important crossroads, this has been a town where many travellers have continued to pause and then pass on to other destinations. Even now the town is still important for commuters, and many residents travel daily to London by train.

The threat of invasion by Spain in the days of Queen Elizabeth I led to Brentwood being used for a new purpose. Somewhere was needed for the mustering of troops and Robert Dudley, Earl of Essex and favourite of the Queen, selected Brentwood as the ideal place in 1588. Men arrived from the Midlands and the eastern counties and prepared to move to the coast, ready for the arrival of the Armada. By late July, 900 horsemen had arrived and somehow the local population coped with this sudden disturbance to their usually quiet lives. Although the Spanish fleet was scattered, there was still fear of invasion from Europe and soldiers assembled in the area again in 1597 and 1599.

A Dancing Actor

It was also in 1599 that a well-known actor, Will Kempe, set out to dance all the way from London to Norwich. His servant carried a supply of goods that could be sold as they travelled and the pair conveniently arrived in Brentwood on market day. The actor was impressed by the size of the crowd that came out to greet him, but large crowds attracted thieves and two cutpurses and their accomplices were arrested and removed to the town whipping post. They were probably taken to the Assize House, an ancient building towards the west end of the High Street. This was eventually demolished and in 1842 an impressive Town Hall took its place. This in turn has now gone and another Town Hall stands in Ingrave Road. The clock from the Victorian Town Hall hangs on the wall of the present building, a reminder of bygone days.

Roads

Inns have always played an important part in the life of the town. Some have long since been demolished, but others remain and will be dealt with in more detail in a later chapter. Coaches used the old Essex Great Road, the highway once used by the Romans, and inns were needed to provide accommodation, food and drink, and also fresh horses as the climb up to the town along Brook Street was notoriously steep. Daniel Defoe described Brentwood, Ingatestone and Chelmsford as being towns full of good inns.

We may complain about the state of our roads in the twenty-first century, but by the early seventeenth century the poor condition of the road between Brentwood and Chelmsford was well known. Deep holes were reported, bad enough to injure a horse or overturn a coach. Something needed to be done, but the cost of repairs was considerable. One solution was a ban on heavy wagons between October and the end of April.

Towards the end of the seventeenth century turnpikes were becoming popular. They raised money that could be used for much needed road improvements. Unfortunately, travellers needed to take care as highwaymen frequented many roads. By 1780 a regular coach passed through Brentwood on its way between London and Ipswich. Before the end of that century, three coaches ran each day between Brentwood and London.

The Return of the Army

The military again came to the town at the time of the American War of Independence. France gave support to America and, in 1778, there were fears that the French might invade Britain. Troops were once more sent to camp on Warley Common and in October King George III and Queen Charlotte arrived so that the monarch could review his troops. A mock battle was staged with 10,000 men involved but after a month the camp broke up, only to reform three times during the next four years. The royal couple stayed at Thorndon Hall with Lord Petre for the duration of their time in the town.

Above left: The Ingatestone mosaic commemorating the visit of Queen Elizabeth I.

Above right: This building, now a shop, was formerly the Lion and Lamb. The old inn signs still appear above the doors.

The Regimental Chapel at Warley Barracks has been preserved.

The French Revolution and the Napoleonic Wars led to the re-establishment of the camp at Warley. Then, around 1805, barracks were constructed at Little Warley. The 2nd Battalion 44th Foot, later to become the Essex Regiment, captured the French eagle standard in 1812 during the Battle of Salamanca. Following this, the eagle was added to the badge of the regiment.

1842 saw more changes to the barracks when they were sold to the East India Co. At this time many of the large houses still to be seen in Brook Street were built for officers and their families. The company did not remain in the town for long and, in 1861, Warley Barracks passed into the hands of the War Office.

The First World War again saw Warley playing an important part in history. Some soldiers moved into the barracks and others were billeted with local families. Still more simply passed through the town on their way to the East Coast and beyond. Coombe Lodge at Warley, now known as the Squirrels Care Centre, was taken over and used as a hospital for the wounded. There were just eighty-three beds but 2,140 soldiers were treated during the years of war. Sadly a number died and their graves can still be seen in the Lawn Road Cemetery. This is a very atmospheric place, with so many of the graves bearing the names, regiments and ages of young men who died as the result of their wounds. Many were Irish.

The barracks continued to be important during the Second World War, with Brentwood once more becoming a town of passage as soldiers stayed for a while or passed through towards the coast. It was used again during the time of National Service, but in 1964 its days as a useful military barracks ended and the site was taken over by the Ford Motor Co. for its European headquarters. The building faces Eagle Way, a reminder of those days when the eagle standard was taken from the French by the Essex-based soldiers.

Ford's head office now stands on the site of the barracks.

Although the main barracks buildings have gone, there are still other reminders of the time when the Army was stationed in Warley. In 1939 the officers' mess had been built on the north side of Eagle Way. Following the closure of the barracks the Sisters of Charity of St Vincent de Paul moved into the building, transferring their hospital from Warley House, an impressive mansion that once stood opposite the Horse and Groom. The new hospital is known as the Marrilac. The Garrison Church, built by the East India Co. in 1857, also still stands facing the massive Ford building. On the opposite side of Eagle Way is Keys Hall, once the gymnasium for the barracks.

The Trains Arrive

We take public transport very much for granted in the twenty-first century, although we often grumble about the inadequacies of the systems. Yet it wasn't until 1840 that the first London to Brentwood train arrived. As Brentwood is on a hill, the station had to be built at the bottom and so is away from the centre of the town. The building of the railway presented the engineers with a number of previously unforeseen problems.

Originally plans were made to bring trains from Shoreditch to Romford, Brentwood, Chelmsford and Colchester. The Eastern Railway Co. had been formed in 1836 and the task of construction was given to John Braithwaite and C.B. Vignoles. The line reached Romford in June 1839 and Brentwood the following year. Five trains a day reached the town and once again travellers arrived, especially soldiers going to the barracks.

At about this time the first fatality occurred. A young man lost his hat when it fell from the train. Somewhat foolishly, he leapt down from the moving carriage in an attempt to retrieve it, but this action cost him his life. This sad event was recorded by the rector of Warley. There was also trouble when a train was derailed close to Brentwood. However, the real problems came when it was needed to extend the line over seven miles of land belonging to Lord Petre. Huge sums were demanded in compensation and it was some time later, following various legal battles, that agreement was finally reached.

Further problems were encountered when a very deep cutting was required and hundreds of navvies were drafted into the town to do the work. Spring water made the sides slip and there was also the need to construct a massive bridge to carry Hartswood Road over the cutting. This enormous feat became known as Seven Arches Bridge. It was built entirely from bricks rescued after the demolition of Mill Green House, a mansion in Ingatestone. Today trains still rush under this mighty structure, with most passengers not realizing the huge engineering challenges encountered during its construction.

A major consideration when a deep cutting is made is what to do with the spoil. In this case, Shenfield Common was nearby and evidence of the solution can be seen amongst the trees where large spoil heaps still exist, making an exciting playground for imaginative children.

A Changing Town

With the new station being built to the south of the town, more people wanted to live close by. A building boom started with Queens Road and New Road being laid out by the early 1840s. Shortly after that, Gresham Road and Rose Valley were also developed. There was once a nursery garden at the junction of Kings Road and Queens Road which belonged to Colonel

Left: The Seven Arches Railway Bridge. (By kind permission of Sylvia Kent)

Below: Shops in Station Parade, *c.* 1980. (By kind permission of Sylvia Kent)

Wilson's Corner and
Spurgeon terrace of shops.

Fielder, who was also the owner of a brewery in Kings Road. Only the Brewery Tap now remains as a reminder of that earlier brewery.

Once soldiers arrived for training at the Warley Barracks, new shops opened to cater for their needs. There was a move away from the supply of farming provisions as this transient population had very different requirements. The majority of the shops at that time were small family businesses.

Other parts of the town were also being developed, especially close to the High Street. Many of the houses at the south end of Ongar Road date from late Victorian or Edwardian times. Alterations have been made to the fronts and backs of many of these properties but, in most cases, the roofs are little changed, although now solar panels and television aerials may be seen. There are also terraced rows of cottages in the roads behind the High Street on both sides. Often these still bear their original date of construction.

One interesting row of shops was built in 1883 by a Mr Spurgeon. These still stand at the north-east corner of the High Street. Sadly the project led to bankruptcy for the builder and many people nicknamed the shops 'Spurgeon's Folly'. This was an unfortunate nickname when you realise the number of other High Street buildings that have long since disappeared, whereas Spurgeon's remain open and very rarely do any of them fall empty.

A New Church

During Queen Victoria's reign the town grew, as did the size of Church congregations. This was the time when the whole household was expected to attend Sunday services, including the servants. For some years the fabric of the High Street chapel had been deteriorating and little was done to stop this from happening. In 1835 it was decided that the building was too dilapidated and small for the needs of the expanding town. The time had come to build a new, larger church.

A nursery garden to the south of the High Street was chosen as the site of the new building and negotiations were completed and the ground cleared. It was decided to name this church, like the chapel, after St Thomas à Becket, the martyr whose pilgrims had once travelled through the town on their way to Canterbury.

James Savage, a well-known architect of that time, designed the new building, complete with a solid-looking tower. It was an impressive-looking structure but, before long, signs of inferior workmanship appeared. The tower proved to be especially vulnerable and, after less than fifty years, was in a state of collapse. The curate at that time was Francis Rhodes, the father of Cecil Rhodes.

A Memorable Fire

With the dawn of a new century many things changed in the town. By 1901 the population had reached almost 5,000, although South Weald still had more inhabitants. Over the previous century more shops had appeared in the High Street and the crossroads at Ingrave Road and Shenfield Road was dominated by Wilson's, a large emporium. The corner still bears the name of the early proprietor, William Wilson, who had acquired the site in 1887. He opened his first shop as a boot and shoe retailer, but expanded his range of goods once he moved into the Ingrave Road store.

It was in 1909 that disaster struck. There was a paint store in the shop and that is where a fire started. The flames spread quickly and before long the whole building was a raging inferno. The heat was so intense that wax dummies melted in the shop windows. The local fire brigade arrived and the numbers of firefighters were soon reinforced by soldiers from Warley Barracks. At the height of the fire, shop windows on the opposite side of the road in Spurgeon's Terrace shattered. This was when the stone of the Hunter Memorial cracked, to be restored some time later.

Wilson's Corner and the High Street.

The old fire station in Hart Street.

All the efforts of the firefighters were in vain; the building was completely destroyed. However, within a year a new shop was rising and, like its forerunner, it was dominated by an imposing clock tower. The general appearance of the building remains the same, although it served for some time as an impressive furniture store and, after several years of lying empty, it now houses several well set-out specialist shops.

The Coming of the Fire Station

In 1902 the town saw the opening of a purpose-built fire station. This was in Hart Street, formerly known as Back Street. Recently a small development of interesting shops in Roper's Yard has been built behind the old fire station. Although they are away from the main High Street, it is well worth walking through this fascinating area and seeing the sort of goods offered for sale.

A much larger and better-equipped fire station in Western Road has now replaced the old one, but the earlier building still retains its former name. For a while it was used as an ambulance station and then as the home of Blue Line Car Hire. It is now a barber's shop and trades under the name of The Headquarters.

Two Friends of the Town

The name of Larkin crops up frequently in the history of the town. The two brothers, John and George, were great benefactors. John Larkin's very individual *Fireside Talks About Brentwood* and *More Fireside Talks* are still a delight to read, with his very personal views on the development of the town. The brothers are remembered for various gifts to Brentwood, including Larkin's

Playing Fields in Ongar Road, the clock on St Thomas' Church, presented in 1923, and a drinking fountain on Shenfield Common. Earlier, in 1910, they also gave an attractive horse trough and drinking fountain which stands in the High Street, close to Wilson's Corner. Although no longer used for its original purpose, it remains a reminder of a bygone age when horses were an important part of the local scene.

An Important Local Employer

In the early years of the twentieth century, the High Street remained a peaceful place with its trees and large houses interspersed with thriving shops.

Selo was one of the town's main employers from the early years of the new century. The company was originally started by Alfred Harman as a photographic business in Peckham, before later moving to Ilford where the dust-free atmosphere was more suitable for this type of work. In 1904 Ilford Ltd (Selo) opened a Brentwood factory in Woodman Road. After a brief closure in 1910, it re-opened and started producing roll film, an important invention superseded only in recent years by the digital camera. The factory was requisitioned by the Army in 1916 and used as a store and only returned to private ownership in 1921.

The firm introduced many new ideas and produced cine, colour and X-ray film of high quality. During the Second World War the company's specialist knowledge was again in demand, especially for aerial reconnaissance film.

Throughout its time in the town, Selo played an important part in local activities. Apart from being an employer of many Brentwoodians, the company had a thriving sports and social club, raised funds for local charities and it even had its own band.

It was in 1983 that the town was shocked to hear that the Woodman Road plant was to close. Many employees accepted retirement or redundancy, while others moved with the company to Mobberley in Cheshire. The following year the site was sold and an estate of 280 houses was built on this valuable land.

War

With the outbreak of war in 1914, Frank D. Simpson, in his *Brentwood in Old Picture Postcards*, recalls the town being transformed into one vast garrison. As well as the barracks at Warley, a military camp was established on Shenfield Common and almost every household had one or more soldiers billeted with them. In addition to Coombe Lodge at Great Warley, a number of other large houses in the area were taken over for the care of the wounded. Hospital blue became a common sight around the town.

A local death is recorded at this time. Nurse Evans had come home on leave from France where she must have been in constant danger. Yet it was while she was in Priests Lane that she was hit by the sole bomb dropped on Shenfield during the First World War. Many of the nearby houses were damaged and windows were shattered by the force of the blast. Brentwood's War Memorial, erected in 1921 at the junction of Middleton Hall Lane and Shenfield Road, records

Above left: The Brentwood War Memorial.

Above right: The Palace cinema in the High Street. (By kind permission of Sylvia Kent)

the names of those from the town lost during both world wars. This memorial was originally planned for the crossroads at Wilson's Corner, but fortunately this idea was abandoned as it would almost certainly have had to be moved with the massive increase in traffic we see today. Over the years the condition of the memorial has deteriorated. It was therefore decided by Brentwood Council in 2009 that restoration work would be undertaken at an estimated cost of £50,000.

The Years Between

1914 saw the opening of the town's first cinema. This was the Electric Palace in the High Street. Twenty years later it was rebuilt as a modern cinema with 1,100 seats. At this time it was renamed the Palace. It eventually closed when a new Sainsbury's was built on the site.

The Parade cinema opened in 1922. This was very close to the railway station and in 1930 it became the first cinema in the town to have 'talkies'. It finally closed in 1940 and was, for some time, used as a warehouse and then as a nightclub. It was finally demolished in the mid-1980s but the name lives on; the Kingsgate office block has been built on the site with the old road name, the Parade, fixed to the wall.

A third cinema came to Brentwood in 1938. Behind the chapel ruins in the High Street had stood a large house which was named The Priory. This had been demolished the year before and the impressive Odeon cinema took its place. It remained a much-loved feature of the town until it too was closed in 1973 and was demolished prior to the building of the Chapel High shopping precinct. The Focus 1 and 2 cinemas were built as part of this new complex.

Above left: The Baytree Shopping Centre.

Above right: The Victorian Town Hall in the High Street. (By kind permission of Sylvia Kent)

However, as the new millennium dawned plans were made to rebuild the precinct without a cinema. This has been renamed the Baytree Centre as two large bay trees grow close to the old chapel.

After extensive discussions, plans are apparently going ahead for a new cinema to be built in William Hunter Way.

The Second World War

Warley Barracks flourished with the outbreak of the Second World War. Brentwood once more became a town of passage as soldiers passed through for training or to set out for overseas postings. Although within twenty-five miles of London, the town was still used for evacuees. 6,000 arrived from London in 1939 to be billeted in houses throughout the town. Unfortunately this did not mean that Brentwood was immune from attack. In fact, there were well over 400 casualties throughout the hostilities, with forty-three fatalities. The people of Brentwood took the war effort seriously. In just two weeks in 1940, enough money was collected from residents to pay for a Spitfire, duly named *Brentwood*.

With the approach of D-Day troops and equipment gathered in local green spaces, including Thorndon Park and Weald Park. These were ideal places for military vehicles to assemble.

Peace came in 1945, but two years later the town was proud to welcome Field Marshal Viscount Montgomery when he visited Warley Barracks. The barracks had played their part in various wars over the years and it was a fitting tribute that they should welcome one of the true heroes of the Second World War.

The Years of Recovery

Recovery from the austere years of war took time, as it did throughout the country, but gradually things began to change. In 1949 electric trains replaced the old steam locomotives. With their sliding doors and smart green paint, many felt they were a great improvement, although others regretted the passing of the old trains with their distinctive smells and sounds.

In August 1952 the first four houses were completed on the East Ham Estate, lying behind Running Waters. The scheme was designed to provide housing for some of those families displaced in the war. Not all the locals liked the idea of what they regarded as an invasion but, by 1954, more than 2,000 had submitted an application for the houses.

The Coronation on 2 June 1953 was a day for celebration. The town was decorated with flags and bunting and there were many street parties. A carnival with bands and colourful floats wound its way through the roads from Little Highwood Hospital, ending up at Brentwood School sports ground. There entertainment was laid on, including sports and a funfair and the day ended with fireworks.

A real sign that the austere days of war were finally passing was the opening in 1955 of the town's first self-service store in the High Street. This was Tesco, to be followed before the end of the decade by Fine Fare and the Co-op.

1957 was an auspicious year in the life of the town as it saw three important royal events. The Duke of Edinburgh opened the Ramsden Research and Development Laboratory at the Selo works in Woodman Road, while the Queen, with the Duke of Edinburgh, opened the new science block at Brentwood School. They also opened the new Council offices, opposite the school in Ingrave Road. These replaced the old Victorian Town Hall in the High Street, which in turn had replaced the earlier Assize House. The Council offices, now the Town Hall, have since been extended and the clock from the High Street building has been placed on the new one, an interesting link with the past. To the south of the building there is another clock. This was donated by the Ford Motor Co. after renovation as it too had historic links with the town, having once hung at Warley Barracks.

The 1960s and '70s saw more demolition and new buildings. Brentwood is divided from outer London by just a few fields constituting the green belt. This land is jealously guarded and, although there are occasional incursions, it means that most new building has to be on brown sites. Sadly this can lead to places of historic interest being lost.

Times of Change

Once pilgrims came to Brentwood by foot or on horseback. In later years, travellers often passed through using the popular stagecoaches. Then the railway brought visitors more swiftly by train. However, October 1986 saw the official opening of the M25. Although some motorists leave at Junction 28 to follow Brook Street into the town, for many more this is simply one more place name to pass on the way to other locations.

Like most parts of the country, Brentwood suffered during the gales of October 1987. Thousands of trees in the area were destroyed, but an inspired way of using the timber was introduced at Thorndon Park. A new visitors' centre was opened the following year using wood from fallen trees. It remains an attractive reminder that something good can come from apparent disaster.

November 1988 saw the opening of the Brentwood Centre in Doddinghurst Road. This huge sports and entertainment complex includes a superb swimming pool. The old open-air one, dating from 1935, was no longer needed and the site became a part of the new Sainsbury's superstore. Now a children's playground has been restored behind the building where the swimming pool once stood.

Many towns now have their own closed circuit television cameras. Some regard them as a great innovation whilst others are less enthusiastic. However, back in 1994, Brentwood was the first town in the country to adopt this method of attempting to keep its streets safe.

The New Millennium

A special clock sponsored by Brentwood Borough Council and the *Brentwood Gazette* ticked away the months, hours and finally seconds until the dawn of a new millennium. The clock was then adapted to become a normal timepiece and became an interesting addition to the High Street. It was removed during the High Street renovations in 2009. Apparently it will again be restored to the High Street, but in a slightly different location.

As the new millennium dawned, fireworks filled the sky over Brentwood. The year 2000 had arrived and the town prepared to meet the new challenges ahead.

3

People and Places

Being close to London but remaining a rural area meant that Brentwood became a desirable place for the wealthy to acquire estates and imposing houses. Today many of those mansions remain, although the majority now serve very different purposes from those for which they were originally intended. Being on a regular stagecoach route and later having its own railway station, the town became even more popular with those looking for a country residence. It also had a reputation for being a very healthy place to live, with good, clean country air.

Marygreen Manor Hotel

Any traveller entering the town today from the M25 must notice the beautiful Marygreen Manor Hotel to the south of Brook Street. A timber-framed house has stood on this site since at least the thirteenth century, so pilgrims visiting Brentwood throughout the Middle Ages must also have been aware of the property, although it has been greatly altered and extended over the years.

Brook Street was a tiny hamlet to the west of Brentwood. To the north of the Essex Great Road was the leper hospital and the master's house. Opposite this was a water mill beside the brook and the moated house, now known as Marygreen Manor. By the fifteenth century the Roper family held the tenancy of the manor and alterations were made. They also held Great Ropers and Little Ropers in Warley. Henry Roper became a yeoman officer and was appointed to 'look after' the young Catherine of Aragon when she first arrived in England. In his time the manor house was further extended and was known as The Place. He died in 1517 and his estate passed to his godson, also Henry Roper.

Robert Wright inherited the tenancy of the moated house on the death of his father in 1551. Robert had married Mary Green, the daughter of a Navestock landowner. They settled in the house which became known as Brook Hall. The estate was renamed the Manor of Marygreen, a name remembered in the present title of the hotel. The last of that branch of the family died in 1723, although other family members remained in the area.

Various owners came and went over the following years until Herbert Swift, his wife Joan, and their three children took over the house and ten acres of land in 1957. During their occupancy of the house they were occasionally visited by descendants of Thomas and Anthony Wright who had emigrated to America some 300 years before. This branch of the family included Orville and Wilbur Wright, the aviation pioneers. The Swift family left for Australia in 1967 when the house was purchased by John Bairstow.

The back of Marygreen Manor Hotel.

In 1967 work started on turning the building into a luxury hotel and restaurant. Extensions were added, but very much in keeping with the style of the old house, which is a Grade II listed building. At that time it was known as the Moat House. In 1993 it came up for sale and was taken over by Paul Pearson and backers. One stipulation was that the name 'Moat House' could no longer be used. Marygreen Manor Hotel was chosen instead, in memory of Mary Roper (née Green) who had lived in the house so many years before.

Weald Hall and Weald Park

It was in 1541, during the reign of Henry VIII, that the king granted the manor of South Weald to Sir Brian Tuke, who set about rebuilding Weald Hall. Following several ownership changes the estate was bought by Anthony Browne, together with the manors of Costed and Calcot. His name is still well remembered in the town. After attending Oxford University he became a lawyer and played an active part in politics, serving under Edward VI, Mary Tudor and Elizabeth I. This was no mean achievement in a time of constant religious turmoil. He was knighted in 1566, the year before his death.

As previously mentioned, Sir Anthony Browne is especially remembered for his involvement in the death of William Hunter and also for the founding of Brentwood School. He was a magistrate at the trial of the local martyr. Some people believe that he might have founded the school as an act of contrition for his part in the death of the nineteen-year-old, but this is purely speculation.

As Sir Anthony died childless, the estate passed to his great-nephew, Wistan Browne. He was an unpopular figure having been involved in the attempt to close the Brentwood Chapel and later tried to seize property of the recently established school. Again he was unsuccessful.

At the time of the Civil War, a later Sir Anthony Browne supported the cause of the ill-fated king. Like others at that sad time in England's history, he ran into considerable debt as he tried to give financial support to the cause of the monarchy. As a result of his many debts he was forced to sell Weald Hall to a lawyer, William Scroggs, and the Browne family faded from the history of Brentwood.

The lake in Weald Park.

Children feeding the deer in Weald Park.

In 1752 Thomas Tower, a London lawyer, bought Weald Hall, which he used as a weekend retreat. However, he did rebuild some of the local almshouses. Christopher Tower was Squire of South Weald from 1810 to 1867. In that time he greatly extended the size of the estate and added Cashmere goats to the animals already grazing the park. Another of his projects involved restoring the Great Hall of the mansion.

The Second World War led to many changes in the area. The military took over a number of large houses throughout the country, and Weald Hall was one of these. The park was used for assembling troops in the run up to D-Day. Damage following the occupation of the house was considerable, and in 1950 the hall was demolished.

The grounds of Weald Hall are now a country park run by Essex County Council. This is a real jewel in the crown of the town with its superb lakes and fine views. The noble families of the past have gone, but this beautiful open area, part of the green belt surrounding the town, can now be enjoyed by everyone and is a fitting memorial to those who developed the land in the past.

Warley Place

Close to the Thatchers Arms in Warley is the entrance to what were once the grounds of Warley Place. This fine mansion with an interesting history stood here until its demolition in 1939. This was the home of Miss Ellen Willmott and, in its heyday, it was surrounded by one of the most notable gardens in the country.

Born to Frederick and Ellen Willmott in August 1858 and named after her mother, Ellen May was their first child. At that time the family lived in London. Her godmother was Helen Tasker of Middleton Hall, Brentwood, a lady who was to have a great influence on the child. Later Rose and Ada Mary were born but, sadly, Ada did not survive childhood. From the age of seven, her godmother gave Ellen a cheque for £1,000 each year on her birthday, a princely sum then and today worth around £15,000. By the time of her twenty-first birthday, Ellen Willmott was a very wealthy young woman.

The crossroads at Warley facing the entrance to Warley Place.

It was in 1875 that Frederick Willmott, by then a prosperous solicitor, decided to move to a more rural area, but one from which he could still easily reach London. With the coming of the railway, Brentwood was the ideal town and Warley Place was the perfect location. The estate had once been held by the Abbess of Barking Abbey and is believed to have contained the sanatorium of the abbey and also the fishponds. Later it came into the ownership of John Evelyn, the diarist.

The Willmott family members were devout Roman Catholics, as was Ellen's godmother. Over the years Ellen keenly supported nearby Holy Cross and All Saints Church, which became known as 'Miss Willmott's church'.

The family quickly settled into their new home and Mrs Willmott and her daughters started planning the garden. Miss Ellen Willmott became a passionate gardener and collector of rare plants, an interest that would stay with her throughout her life.

Following the marriage of her sister and the death of her parents, Ellen developed her beloved garden even more. She travelled abroad collecting unusual plants and became one of the most noted horticulturalists of her time. There were more than 100,000 species and varieties of plants, cared for by a staff of 100 gardeners. Even royalty visited her Brentwood home, including Princess Victoria and Edward, Prince of Wales, later followed by George V and Queen Mary.

The costs of running the house and gardens were astronomical. Money ran out and many of the staff had to be dismissed. Valuables, carefully collected over the years, were sold to raise money. The house and grounds deteriorated until, in September 1934, at the age of seventy-six, Ellen Willmott died alone and was found by one of her few remaining servants. Her end may seem sad, but her name lives on in the titles of many of the plants she developed at Warley Place. The grounds are now cared for by the Essex Wildlife Trust.

De Rougemont Manor

Evelyn Heseltine is mentioned in Chapter 4 as the man who built the beautiful Church of St Mary the Virgin at Great Warley. This alone was a remarkable achievement, but his name is remembered for other philanthropic work too.

In 1867 he and his wife Emily bought Goldings Cottage. Over the years the original building has been greatly extended. The family also decided to turn around the entrance to the house, so that instead of facing the road it overlooked Upminster Common. Many local people were employed both inside and outside the house. Although they lived close to Warley Place and were there at the same time as Ellen Willmott, the two families do not appear to have had much social contact.

After the deaths of both Evelyn and his wife, the house passed to their daughter, Murial. She was the wife of Major General Cecil De Rougemont, a hero of the Boer War. Sadly, Murial lost both her sons; one died young and the other was killed in the Second World War. This meant that following her death the house was sold to two local businessmen and became the New World Country Club. Ian Hilton later bought out his partner and the club was renamed the New World Inn. Once again the building was redesigned so that the main entrance faced the road. Following a devastating fire and the rebuilding of the property it received yet another name, De Rougemont Manor, after Murial, the daughter of Evelyn and Emily Heseltine.

De Rougemont Manor Hotel, formerly the home of Evelyn Heseltine.

Brentwood School owes much to the generosity of Evelyn Heseltine. In 1910 he was responsible for buying Roden House for the school. As Chairman of the Governors, he ensured that the school grounds were greatly extended. Close to the school are the Shen Place Almshouses which were opened by Evelyn Heseltine in 1910, although the tall chimneys make the building appear older.

Middleton Hall

Helen Tasker, godmother to Ellen Willmott, was born in 1823. Her father, Joseph Tasker, was a wealthy London businessman. Joseph and his wife had two children, Helen and Joseph Louis. Sadly, their mother died when they were still young and Joseph did not survive long into adulthood, dying at sea at the age of twenty-four. Joseph senior owned property in London and also Middleton Hall, a fine mansion standing in extensive grounds. His financial skills made him an extremely wealthy man. When he died in 1861, his property and fortune passed to Helen who, like her parents, was a staunch Roman Catholic. The road outside the house was known as Tasker Lane in Victorian times, but it is now called Middleton Hall Lane.

Helen remained unmarried but was devoted to her goddaughter. She must have been delighted when the Willmott family moved into Warley Place. She also gave keen financial support to the Roman Catholic Church and, as a result of this, Pope Pius IX bestowed on her the title of Countess in 1870.

Middleton Hall, now Brentwood Preparatory School.

The shock resulting from a burglary at Middleton Hall may well have contributed to the death of Countess Tasker in January 1888. There is a story told that she jumped from a balcony but, with her religious convictions, this is unlikely. Another tale says that her ghost appears whenever alterations are made to the house. Following her death, Middleton Hall passed to a cousin and it was sold in 1897, thus ending the association with the Tasker family.

The mansion still stands, but it is no longer a private residence. In 1949 it was taken over by Brentwood Preparatory School. As need has arisen, extra buildings have been added on the site, but the main building retains all its earlier beauty.

Thorndon Hall and Thorndon Park

We have already seen that Sir William Petre, who lived during the sixteenth century, was the founder of the oldest noble family resident in Essex. After some involvement in politics he bought the manor of Gynge Abbess in 1538. This had previously belonged to Barking Abbey. He demolished the existing Abbess Hall and replaced it with Ingatestone Hall. By 1545 he became a Privy Councillor and served under Edward VI; he also served under Mary I and then her sister, Elizabeth, which was no mean achievement in those difficult times.

Following his father's death in 1572, Sir William's only surviving son, John, bought West Horndon Hall, which dated from 1414. The next twenty years were spent rebuilding the

old house and it became known as Thorndon Hall, the principal seat of the family. John was knighted in 1576 and later became the first Baron Petre.

The 9th Lord Petre decided to build a new mansion in 1764. This was one mile to the north of the old hall, which was then demolished. The design of the new house was by James Paine, with an impressive portico by Giacomo Leoni. The construction took six years and the beautiful grounds were laid out by Capability Brown.

The owner of this impressive house was honoured in October 1778 when King George III and Queen Charlotte stayed for two days. This was a very expensive time for the Petres, but it was especially welcomed by Roman Catholics in the area as it was the first time since the days of Elizabeth I that a reigning monarch had stayed with a Roman Catholic.

Disaster struck in 1878 when fire gutted the building, causing severe damage. For the next 100 years the hall remained semi-derelict. Then, in the 1920s, Thorndon Golf Club was established in the grounds and used part of the hall. Finally, well over a century after the devastating fire, Thomas Bates Ltd obtained permission to convert the ruined building into luxury apartments. Phoenix-like, Thorndon Hall has now been reborn and is once again a well-cared-for gem.

The country park surrounding the old building is open to the public and includes the interesting visitors' centre, created from fallen trees from the devastating 1987 gales. Many nature-related events take place in the park throughout the year.

Ingatestone Hall

This beautiful old house is, like Thorndon Hall, a Grade I listed building. As mentioned above, William Petre, who was knighted in 1543, bought the manor of Gynge Abbess complete with Abbess Hall. The hall was then demolished to be replaced with Ingatestone Hall. He worked energetically for the Crown and acquired a huge holding of land, much of which was in Essex. In July 1561, Queen Elizabeth I was a guest at the hall; this visit was commemorated in a mosaic to be found in the main street through Ingatestone. Sir William died in 1572.

Following the fire of 1878, Thorndon Hall was left in its ruined state and the family returned once more to Ingatestone Hall.

Essex Lunatic Asylum

This terrifying name was given to the massive complex of buildings erected in the 1850s, later to be known as Warley Hospital. It was in 1849 that William Kavanagh, the owner of the Brentwood Hall Estate, sold eighty-six acres of his land for the building of a new mental hospital. The first part of the building to be completed was ready for occupation in 1853. Designed by H.E. Kendall in the Gothic style, new patients must have found their first view of the asylum extremely frightening.

At one time, around 2,000 inhabitants were housed in the building. Attitudes towards mental health have changed greatly over the years, but from early times the inhabitants were encouraged to work around the hospital and their jobs might have included gardening or laundry work. There was also a neighbouring farm where some were employed.

In recent years there has been a move away from having large mental hospitals. Many of the old buildings have now been demolished and where once there must have been considerable sorrow and trauma, there is now a pleasing housing development and school. Part of the main building remains, but this has also been converted into interesting apartments.

Brizes

The first manor house of Brizes, Kelvedon Hatch, was built around 1498. The owner at that time was a London mercer, Thomas Bryce. In 1515 it was acquired by a London alderman, Sir John Allen. As has already been noted, many of the mansions in the area were owned by wealthy men who could easily reach the city of London.

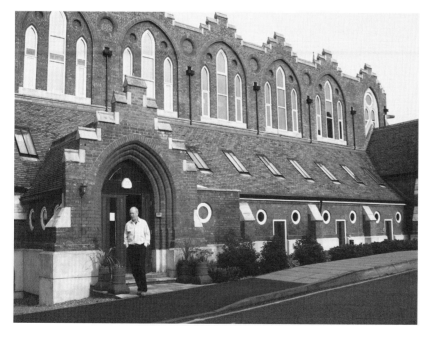

The old chapel at Warley Hospital.

The house changed ownership on several occasions until, by the time of the Civil War, it was in the hands of Ralph Pettus. Like a number of other landowners in the area, his support of the king had disastrous results. His estate was sequestrated and he needed to raise £800 if it was to be redeemed. This proved to be impossible and he lost the property.

The mansion that can be seen today standing in beautiful grounds dates from 1720. It has now been taken over by the Peniel School and still retains the impressive staircase that was included in reconstruction during the eighteenth century.

Shenfield Place

1689-90 saw the building of this fine old house. It was designed by the architect Robert Hook, an associate of Sir Christopher Wren. For a number of years it was owned by the well-known Courage family before passing to the Baymans. It was auctioned in the 1920s and at that time sold for £11,555.

In more recent years an estate of much sought-after homes has been built in the grounds, but the house itself remains. It is now a nursing and retirement residence.

Rochetts

Born in 1735, John Jarvis came from a family with naval connections, and his father was an Admiralty solicitor. When he was fourteen years old, John decided to join the Navy and signed on as an able seaman. This might seem surprising, but the only help he received from his father was a donation of £20. However, hard work on the part of the young man soon led to promotion.

By 1782 he was commander of the eighty-gun *Foudroyant* and one night he captured the seventy-four-gun French ship *Pegase*. This resulted in him being made a Knight of Bath and later an admiral.

Rochetts in South Weald was held by Sir Thomas Parker, Chief Baron of the Exchequer. In 1783 John Jarvis had married his cousin, Martha, the daughter of Sir Thomas, and the couple lived at Rochetts until the older man died in 1784. The house then passed to Martha and the building was soon extended.

1797 was a memorable year for John Jarvis. With just fifteen ships he managed to defeat twenty-seven Spanish ships that had intended joining the French fleet in an attempt to invade England. Four of the Spanish ships were taken and many others were badly damaged and fled off Cape St Vincent. The delighted king rewarded his admiral with the title of Earl St Vincent, a name still used by the hamlet where Rochetts stands. He was also rewarded with a pension of £3,000 per year, a massive sum at that time. When ill health caused his retirement from active service, Earl St Vincent became First Lord of the Admiralty.

Following his retirement, John continued to live at Rochetts and among his guests at the house was the Prince of Wales, later George IV. In 1821 the king made his old friend Admiral of the Fleet. John Jarvis had always been an extremely energetic and organised man. With more time on his hands, he turned his attention to the estate. This often made life difficult for those

The Old County Court House, dating from 1849, is now a private clinic. At the time of the case between the Tower family and John Jarvis, the old Assize House was still standing.

around him, including his neighbours. In 1816 he came into conflict with the Tower family of Weald Hall. A case was brought against him for cutting some underwood. The Towers won, but the legal expenses came to over £3,000.

Earl St Vincent died in 1823 and the house was later occupied by Octavius Coope, a member of the well-known Romford brewing family.

Old House

In the past there were a number of large, privately owned houses in the tree-lined High Street. The majority of these were occupied by the doctors, lawyers and bankers of the town, but they are mainly just memories now as new shops and offices have taken their place. One survival is Old House. Standing close to Wilson's Corner in Shenfield Road, this creeper-covered building remains, although in the past it has been known by other names and has served many functions. It has been called Shenfield Villa and even the Red Lion as it was, at one time, one of the many coaching inns to be found in the town. Its present name was only adopted late in the nineteenth century.

The exact date of the building is uncertain. It is known to have been standing by 1748 and was constructed in two parts of red brick. The first tenant recorded was Charles White, who died in 1753. Spacious grounds and a paddock were to be found at the rear of the building, although this is now hard to imagine as they have long since disappeared beneath a concrete car park and modern buildings.

A more recent owner of the house was Isaac Rist, who bought the property in 1876, and whose family was well known for owning several High Street shops. In 1918 the building was leased to Brentwood School to be used as a boarding house. One notable boarder in the 1920s was Sir Hardy Amies. Then in 1930 James Hough, headmaster of Brentwood School, bought Old House for the school but stipulated that any rent paid must be used to provide school pupils with scolarships to Oxford and Cambridge.

Old House.

A new phase in the life of Old House came in 1939. It was leased by the school to the London Hospital and was used as a hostel for nurses in training at the London Annex as it adjoined Highwood Hospital. This situation lasted until 1946 when the house returned once more to the control of Brentwood School and was used as the preparatory school and a boarding house.

Change came again in 1966. The house was sold to the Post Office and the massive telephone exchange was built at the rear, but this situation was short-lived. In 1971 Brentwood Council paid £40,000 to buy the house and following considerable conversion it was opened as the Brentwood Arts and Community Centre, a useful addition to the amenities of the town.

Pilgrims Hall

Perhaps it is appropriate to finish this chapter with a look at the history of a house named Pilgrims Hall. This elegant mansion lies beside the Ongar Road. It was originally built early in the nineteenth century by Emanuel Dias Santos, a Portuguese Roman Catholic priest. He was greatly involved in the growth of Roman Catholicism in Brentwood. Over the years it has been extended to become the imposing building that can be seen today.

The hall was, at one time, used as a boarding school and one of the head boys was Samuel Beeton, later the husband of Isabella, the forerunner of writers of popular cookery books. The first of these was published in 1861. Later it again became a private house and the well-known lawyer James Lawrence lived there with his family in the early years of the twentieth century when it was a typical country residence, yet still close enough to London to make daily travel a possibility.

It was in 1968 that Pilgrims Hall was sold to become a Christian training centre. The name was changed to Fellowship House, but it has since reverted to Pilgrims Hall once again whilst remaining a Christian retreat centre.

4

Churches
and Inns

It may seem rather odd to put churches and inns together, but as we have seen pilgrims travelling towards Canterbury would have searched for places of worship and also for somewhere safe to obtain food and shelter for the night. The chapel in the High Street would have dealt with their spiritual needs and many new inns sprang up along their route to cater for their bodily needs. The tradition of having many places for refreshment continues in Brentwood. At the time of writing there are twenty-seven cafés, restaurants and public houses in the High Street alone, which doesn't include takeaways and a number of fast-food shops.

St Thomas' Chapel

St Thomas' Chapel has played a vital part in the history of Brentwood. We have already heard some of the stories from its chequered history. In Victorian times it was thought to be too small for the needs of the growing town and a new church was planned. In its later years it served briefly as a National School for boys. In more recent times, railings have been erected to give the ruin some protection and further restoration was embarked upon in 2008. It is still used for Easter services, a living link to those earlier times. As Brentwood develops in the future it is hoped that the area around this ancient building will become a real focal point of the newly paved High Street.

The White Hart

An early inn is believed to have been on the north side of the Essex Great Road from the chapel. This would have served the needs of the pilgrims and have been popular with them as it was so close to the chapel. The building that now stands on the site is thought to date back to the fifteenth and sixteenth centuries, with parts thought to be from 1480. There have been various developments over the years. Built around a courtyard with an open gallery above, it is easy to imagine Shakespeare's plays being performed in such a setting.

Opposite above: The High Street chapel. (© Frances Clamp)

Opposite below: The courtyard of the White Hart, 2004.

Left: Firemen at the White Hart (Sugar Hut Restaurant) following the fire of 2009.

When the courtyard was excavated, some pottery was unearthed dating from the thirteenth century. It is believed that this is where Richard II stayed when visiting the town to deal with the aftermath of the Peasants' Revolt. In fact, the inn took its name from his emblem of a white hart. In later years the White Hart became a popular coaching inn. There were stables under the gallery and access for coaches through a wide arch.

Cornelius Butler was a well-known and respected doctor in the town between 1812 and 1871. It was in 1815 that both he and the White Hart played their part in history, when he went there to announce the British victory at the Battle of Waterloo.

During the nineteenth century, the White Hart was the headquarters for the Conservatives, whilst the Liberals used the nearby Lion and Lamb. Everything got out of hand during the 1874 election. The Liberals had hired a German band to march along the High Street. As they reached the White Hart members of the other party charged. A fight followed and several broken bones were reported. The members of the band wisely made a hasty exit. As a result of this affray, the Riot Act was read and the town's taverns closed for a period of time.

The White Hart is now a Grade II listed building, although the gallery is no longer open and a third floor has been added to the original structure. Early in the twenty-first century a new name appeared on the inn sign. The White Hart disappeared to be replaced by Sugar Hut Village. Protests followed and a small board has now been added below the larger one bearing the older name to act as a reminder of a very important part of Brentwood's history.

St Thomas' Church porch.

Early one Sunday evening in September 2009, a fire broke out in the old building, though fortunately before the arrival of customers. It spread rapidly upwards through the three storeys and flames burst through the roof, causing considerable damage. Ten fire crews arrived to deal with the flames. It is believed that the fire started in a stairwell. As much of the building is made of timber, it is lucky that the fire crews dealt with the blaze so efficiently and managed to keep the fire contained. At the time of writing, the cause of the blaze is still unknown.

St Thomas the Martyr

As the fabric of the old chapel deteriorated there was a move to find a suitable site for a much larger church. This was to be given the same name as the old one. A former nursery to the south of the High Street was chosen as the ideal site. A design by James Savage, a well-known architect, was chosen and the new building was completed in 1835, although, as noted previously, less than half a century later it was in a state of severe disrepair.

It was decided to replace the whole structure and soon plans for a new building were underway. This time the architect was Mr E.C. Lee and his design was in the Victorian Gothic style. The tower was completed in 1887, surmounted by a spire that is a landmark which can be seen for many miles. During the Second World War the tower was used by the Home Guard as a lookout post.

One of the main features outside the building is the west porch. This is richly carved and shows the four evangelists, two on each side of the door. Beneath his feet each one has his own symbol: an angel or man for St Matthew; an ox for St Luke; a lion for St Mark; and an eagle for St John. Above the door a carved tympanum shows Christ in Glory and, below this, a tablet shows the wise and foolish virgins. It is hardly surprising that there are also two panels showing the murder of St Thomas à Becket. Sadly, in recent years it has been necessary to install railings to protect the porch from vandalism.

It is well worth visiting the interior of this impressive building, where the roof soars above the nave. Over the years there have been many donations from worshippers to beautify the building.

The Golden Fleece and the Nags Head

A Harvester restaurant now occupies the Golden Fleece at the bottom of the Brook Street hill. The majority of diners probably know little of the history of this fascinating building. It is in fact one of the oldest in the town. In 1201 it is known that a leper hospital stood close by, near the present Spital Lane.

The Brook Street hill must have presented a real challenge to the stagecoaches that later passed regularly through the town. Fresh horses would have been needed to undertake this part of the journey and the Golden Fleece would have been one of the inns able to cope with this need.

On the corner of Nags Head Lane stands another old inn, the Nags Head. Believed to date from the mid-eighteenth century, this was another coaching inn dealing with the many travellers who passed along the Essex Great Road. It has had a modern extension added but the eastern part of the building is original. The restaurant is run by the Premier Country Dining Group.

The Sir Charles Napier public house was a well-known landmark at the top of Brook Street hill. It was demolished in 2009 during the High Street road improvement scheme.

The Roman Catholic Cathedral

The Roman Catholic faith has always been strong in Brentwood, with a number of leading families continuing to uphold their beliefs after the Reformation. It was often extremely dangerous to follow the old ways, but those willing to take the risk were able to encourage others.

Quieter times followed the years of turmoil and, in 1837, Lord Petre felt able to give land in the Ingrave Road for the building of a Roman Catholic church. This was to be St Helen's and there was room for a congregation of over 200. By the 1850s the number of worshippers had risen to over 500 and a new building was necessary. This was erected on an adjacent site in the Gothic style in 1861.

1917 was the year Rome decided that Essex needed a new diocese and St Helen's became the Brentwood Roman Catholic Cathedral. Congregations continued to grow in size and by the early 1970s, it was realised that more space was needed. In 1974 a new extension was added to the north side of the Gothic church to form a multi-purpose building. Yet after just fifteen years it was realised that there were structural problems in the new building, reminiscent of those that had existed in the first church built in St Thomas' Road. The cost of repairs would have been astronomical so it was finally decided that a new cathedral must be built. The architect Quinlin Terry was commissioned to undertake the work, which was started in 1989 and completed two years later. It is built in the Classical style, influenced by early Italian Renaissance and English Baroque. Part of the old Gothic church of 1861 was also retained as the south aisle. The cathedral was dedicated by Cardinal Basil Hume.

The inside of the building is striking, with light coming from many windows and chandeliers. There are also a number of unusual features, including a central altar with an octagonal lantern above and an eight-sided font with the basin carved in cruciform shape.

This dramatic cathedral stands on the west side of Ingrave Road with Brentwood School to the east. With their gold-leaf-topped railings, these two buildings make an impressive entry to the town from the south.

The Roman Catholic cathedral.

The Black Horse at
Pilgrims Hatch.

The Black Horse

The Black Horse at Pilgrims Hatch was recorded as an inn and bakery as early as the 1620s. For those travelling from the north towards Canterbury, this would have been a welcome stopping place. The original building was a small hall with a crossing at the northern end. Later in the same century, an extension was added in the form of a southern wing.

This is a very attractive building and it has grown in popularity over the years, noted for its excellent food. Then, in 1999, disaster struck. A fire broke out and quickly spread. By the next day charred beams could be seen jutting skywards from the gutted remains, a sad sight for those who had enjoyed the comforts of this fine old inn. It looked as if the Black Horse would never rise again from the ashes.

In a remarkably short time, fencing appeared to shield the ruin and rebuilding commenced. With very careful restoration the whole structure was restored to its former glory. In May 2000 the doors reopened to the public looking just as it had before, the only difference being the safety precautions required in the new millennium – precautions that were unheard of when the first travellers enjoyed the hospitality of this ancient inn.

The Brentwood Baptist Church

The first meetings of the Brentwood Baptist Church took place in 1884 in the Town Hall. The preacher at that time was a student, William Walker. By October 1885 a new chapel was built. That early building was 30ft by 60ft, with a small porch at the front, and became known as a 'tin tabernacle', a method of building popular in the 1880s, although services were apparently very noisy when it rained! In March 1886 there was the first baptismal service for three people, a very important event for the early congregation.

The Baptist Church, Kings Road.

Unfortunately the building proved to be unsatisfactory and the worshippers left in 1910. Two years later it was sold to the Conservative Club and the money raised from the sale was eventually used to buy the site at the corner of Kings Road and Kings Chase in April 1914. In the meantime, Somerset Hall was used for all meetings and services. Then, with the country at war, Somerset Hall was requisitioned for Army use, so the church had to return once more to the Town Hall. Although by February 1915 the church meeting had accepted the plans for the new building, problems were soon encountered. The government imposed a ban on all new building unless it was connected to the war effort. Prayer meetings were held by the worried congregation. Then, just a fortnight later, the ban was lifted. The foundation stone was finally laid by Sir John McClure on Whit Monday, 24 May 1915, and the official opening ceremony took place in September 1915. A porch was added in 1921 and this was replaced in 1986 in a larger form. Apart from that, the outside of the building has changed little in appearance since those early days.

In recent years, the Brentwood Baptist Church has thrived and played an active part in interdenominational activities in the town.

The Gardeners Arms

Hart Street runs parallel with, but to the south of, the High Street. This used to be known as Back Street and it was here that many merchants had their accommodation during the Middle Ages. (See Chapter 1 for more information on the archaeological discoveries made during the excavations in the millennium year.)

Close to where these discoveries were made stands the Gardeners Arms. We know that an alehouse stood on this site as early as 1262, and this would undoubtedly have been used by some of the pilgrims and other travellers. However, that is not the building that we see today. The present Gardeners Arms is believed to date from 1762, although at one time it served as the local workhouse. In fact, with a rapidly growing population it had to be enlarged in 1805, but it quickly outgrew this extension and in 1828 it was again extended.

According to one local legend, the public house takes its name from a gardener who worked on the adjacent estate. He proved to be one of the landlord's keenest customers and is still remembered, although not by name. The garden in which he worked later became a car park, but has now been redeveloped for apartments.

St Mary the Virgin, Great Warley

This church is one of the most picturesque buildings in Brentwood and is built in the Art Nouveau style. The first church to be built at Great Warley goes back to at least 1247, but all traces have long since disappeared. The ancient building was a brick construction and stood close to the Manor House, later known as Pound House. The site was about 300yds south of the Southend Arterial Road, but over the years the village moved northwards towards Brentwood. This move gained momentum after the establishment of the military camp at Warley. A church was needed to deal with the spiritual needs of those who had settled close to the camp. Christ Church at Warley was completed in 1861 for this purpose.

St Mary the
Virgin at
Great Warley.

It was in 1876 that a young stockbroker, Evelyn Heseltine, and his wife Emily (Minnie) bought Goldings Cottage, a small two-up, two-down dwelling in Warley Street. Later the family became major landowners in the area and also local philanthropists. Over the coming years the house was greatly extended. More recently it was converted into the New World Hotel, now renamed De Rougemont Manor.

It was in April 1901 that the rector announced at the Easter vestry meeting that Evelyn Heseltine had offered the princely sum of £5,000 towards the building of a new church. He also gave the land on which it would be erected. The offer was gladly accepted and Mrs Heseltine laid the foundation stone on 5 July 1902. The design and furnishings for the new church were put in the hands of Mr W. Reynolds-Stephens, while the architect appointed was Mr C. Harrison Townsend. The church was to be built in memory of Arnold Heseltine, younger brother of Evelyn. Just two years later, on 1 June 1904, the new church was consecrated. Entry to the churchyard is through an impressive Grade II listed lych-gate. This carries a carved text by Eric Gill, a sculptor and member of the Artworkers' Guild. The design of the gate was also by Charles Harrison Townsend.

From the outside this is a fairly small building with a round apse at the Sanctuary end and a tower and spire surmounted by a gold-leafed dove holding an olive branch. The churchyard is behind the church, well away from the road, with amazing views over the surrounding countryside.

The building is entered through a porch with unusual double doors. One is wide and the other narrow. For anyone unprepared for the splendour of the interior of the church, the first sight is breathtaking. Silver, gilt, aluminium and mother of pearl are to be found in profusion, yet just one type of wood is present – walnut. Symbolism abounds. The rood screen, designed by William Reynolds-Stephens, has six bronze rose trees and these are repeated in the reredos behind the altar. There are shell flowers and red glass fruits that catch the light, especially when candles are lit. Madonna lilies are a popular motif used in the decoration.

The baptistery area is at the back of the church, with two bronze angels, standing one on each side of the baptismal bowl. It is impossible here to give more than a brief description of the many treasures to be found within this amazing church. The windows are typical of Art Nouveau design. In the sanctuary two of these windows show angels guarding the sacraments. At the west end of the church is a large rose window in bold colours. Sadly this is a replacement for the original, which was shattered by a bomb in 1940. The windows in the nave were also damaged at the same time, but fortunately the building remained intact.

The church has faced vandalism and theft over the years. Brass candelabra, which once stood on the altar, were stolen in 1974 and a sundial was destroyed in 1995. Because of this, the doors can no longer be left open at all times; what a sad reflection on the attitudes of some people in the twenty-first century. However, such incidents are carried out by the few. Great Warley Church is a Grade I listed building. It has appeared on three different television programmes, which made it a popular place for visitors.

In 1904 Evelyn Heseltine wanted to found a church built to the Glory of God. His gift to future generations will surely be seen as one of the great British architectural achievements of the early twentieth century.

The Brewery Tap.

The Brewery Tap

This small public house on the corner of Primrose Hill and Kings Road was previously a working brewery with two deep wells providing the fresh water. One of these wells was situated where there is now an attractive courtyard behind the property. Dating from the 1860s, there were once some tied cottages on Primrose Hill for the brewery workers. What was formerly the brewery is now used for other purposes. Only the original tap room survives, giving the inn its name.

St Andrew's Methodist Church, Herongate

This is sometimes mistaken for an Anglican church, but in fact it is on the Methodist circuit. Originally it was Church of England but, being close to St Nicholas' Church, Ingrave, it was unable to support a congregation and so was taken over by the Methodists approximately forty years ago. The church was first opened on St Andrew's Day more than 125 years ago and was known as a 'chapel of ease' as it was too far for many villagers to walk to the parish church. It is now owned by the Methodists on a covenant so that if they stop using it at any time in the future, it will return to the Church of England. The area around also belongs to the church, including the allotments.

The George and Dragon, Mountnessing

This interesting building first opened its doors in 1769. It stands on the old Roman road and was probably originally built to cater for coaching traffic travelling between London and Colchester and beyond.

For a number of years the restaurant was part of the Beefeater chain, but early in 2009 it was closed and underwent complete refurbishment and restoration. It reopened in April 2009, being described in the brochures as a stylish country pub and eating house. The restaurant is now run by the Premier Country Dining Group under the umbrella of Landmark Leisure

St Peter's Church, South Weald

During his ill-fated reign, King Harold set up a foundation of secular canons at Waltham. The endowment included South Weald and what was later to become Brentwood. In fact, the canons still held South Weald when the Domesday Book was compiled, but 'Burnt Wood', later to be known as Brentwood, received no mention.

St Peter's Church porch.

There was known to be a church at South Weald by around 1150, but very little of that building remains following enthusiastic reconstruction during Victorian times. There is, however, still an interesting Norman arch leading into the church. This is supported by columns with carved, zigzag decoration. The tympanum above the door has squares, each cut into two triangles with a typical Norman dog-tooth pattern above.

An attractive lych-gate leads into the churchyard surrounding the building. These gates were once known as 'coffin gates', and it was here that the corpse could be placed whilst awaiting the arrival of the priest. At the west end of the building is a fine tower dating back to the early sixteenth century. During the annual flower festival it is possible to climb to the top of this tower to see the stunning views over the surrounding countryside.

Much of the Victorian rebuilding happened when Charles Belli was the vicar. He was a wealthy gentleman who used his considerable personal fortune to finance a number of building projects around Brentwood.

All Saints, Doddinghurst

This is an interesting church with an associated priest house. The south doorway, which has a dog-toothed ornament, and the nave date back to the thirteenth century. Other additions were made in the fifteenth century, including the nave roof. There were further alterations in the seventeenth century and again in Victorian times when there was extensive restoration.

Outside, much of the building is of flint and there is a fine shingled spire, typical of many Essex churches. Church Lane, where the building stands, is fairly quiet although the hall on the opposite side of the road is busy and offers good parking.

Brentwood United Reformed Church

It was in 1755 that a Congregational church was opened in Warley Lane, now renamed Kings Road. The building remained in use until 1847, when it was pulled down and a new church built in New Road. Now the only reminder of the old church is a small graveyard in front of the Océ Building. Late in the 1970s and early '80s, considerable work was done on the interior of the North Road building and services are now held upstairs. The ground floor is in constant use for many church-related activities.

The Swan Inn

This is one of the older public houses to be found in Brentwood High Street. The name is associated with William Hunter, the nineteen-year-old martyr, although whether this, or another building of the same name, was the place where the youth spent his last night is open to debate. Certainly some believe that the building is haunted. Visual sightings have been claimed by those working and sleeping in the pub. One such manifestation is said to be of a farrier or

St George's outside pulpit.

blacksmith, possibly killed in an accident involving a horse. Another is of an elderly woman named Sarah who apparently walks between two of the bedrooms.

St George the Martyr Church, Brentwood

This unusual church stands on the Ongar Road and dates from the 1930s. John Larkin, who did so much for Brentwood, left money in his will for a new church to be built. The architects chosen were Messrs Crowe and Careless, and also heavily involved was a local man, Lawrence King. He had been born in the town and attended Brentwood School. St George's was his first church, although later he was involved in other notable ecclesiastical building work. He is also remembered for designing the Borough coat of arms. The foundation stone of the church was laid in 1933, with the opening of the new building being in 1934. Money ran out before completion so the west end was a temporary structure that has now been replaced.

The contrast between St Mary the Virgin at Warley and St George the Martyr is great. The latter is minimalist in design, although it also looks back to the architecture of Ancient Rome. The lofty ceiling gives a feeling of great space. Outside, facing towards the town, is an open-air pulpit, an interesting feature seen by all those travelling along the busy Ongar Road. Volunteers work hard in the gardens surrounding the building and they are regularly mentioned in the list of prize winners of Brentwood in Bloom.

5

Around Brentwood

South Weald

As we have seen, South Weald once dominated the area known today as Brentwood. However, Brentwood has now grown from its humble beginnings, leaving South Weald as a quiet village close to its ancient church.

Before the coming of the Normans, King Harold had set up a foundation of secular canons at Waltham, with South Weald as part of the endowment. In the Domesday Book it is recorded that South Weald had two manors, one where the village now stands, with the other to the north and north-east and known as Calcott or Caldecot.

A church existed in South Weald by around 1150 and a century later it had prospered enough for new building work to be undertaken, with the chancel being rebuilt and a north aisle added.

By the thirteenth century it was felt that a chapel was needed for the pilgrims travelling through Brentwood, as South Weald was too far. Richard, the vicar of South Weald, had to agree to the new building, and this could only happen after he was satisfied that the chapel would in no way affect the Mother Church. The chapel, dedicated to St Thomas à Becket, was probably built in 1221, but the chaplain was not allowed to offer Holy Communion or confession to local parishioners. He also had to rely on offerings from the pilgrims and other visitors for his income and could not expect to be supported by the parish.

Leaping forward in time, the Dissolution of the Monasteries in the reign of Henry VIII led to great changes throughout the land. The king granted the manor of South Weald to Sir Brian Tuke in 1541. He rebuilt Weald Hall and the manor was later sold to Anthony Browne, a figure who has already been discussed.

When the Civil War broke out in 1642, the fourth Anthony Browne supported Charles I. His loyalty cost him dearly and he was forced to sell Weald Hall. After several other owners the hall was acquired by a London lawyer, Thomas Tower, in 1752 and his descendants continued to play an important part in the life of South Weald and Brentwood into the twentieth century.

The Church of St Peter, South Weald, was much altered in Victorian times and Weald Hall was demolished after the Second World War, but the park that once surrounded it remains. It is open to the public and is a real asset to the town.

Above left: The font in St Peter's Church, South Weald.

Above right: Warley, looking towards the High Street. (By kind permission of Sylvia Kent)

Warley

At the time of the compilation of the Domesday Book, Warley consisted of two manors. One was known as Great Warley or Warley Magna, and the other as Abbess Warley after the Abbess of Barking who held the land. Brentwood and the surrounding area had always been regarded as extremely healthy, being well above the Essex marshes to the south. For this reason, in about 1400, the Abbess of Barking decided to build a sanatorium at Great Warley with a fishpond close by. This was the later site of Warley Place.

Brentwood and its surrounding villages were heavily involved in the Peasants' Revolt in the late fourteenth century. When an assize was held at Chelmsford to deal with the men concerned, at least one was known to have come from Warley.

Poaching was often reported during the Middle Ages and beyond. For many people of those times meat was a rare luxury, so it is hardly surprising that some tried to supplement the diets of their families, although the punishments for those caught were harsh. In 1565 fifteen men were charged with this offence, the majority coming from Great Warley. This is perhaps surprising as the village could only claim fifty-nine residents in total in 1671.

In 1649 the diarist John Evelyn is known to have bought the manor of Great Warley. He attended manorial meetings, although apparently he did not live at Warley Place. He sold the property in 1655, claiming that the taxes he was forced to pay were too high. How little attitudes have changed over the years! It is claimed that he planted both the Spanish chestnuts and the early English crocuses in the grounds of Warley Place.

In 1875 Warley Place was bought by Frederick Willmott, a London solicitor. With his wife and two daughters he soon settled down to enjoy the country life, although he was still able to travel easily to London. His eldest child, Ellen, loved their new home, especially the garden. She later inherited the house and developed an internationally recognised skill as a horticultural expert, introducing many new plants, a number of which still bear her name. The house was demolished in 1939 and for many years the garden was completely neglected. In 1977 the grounds were leased to the Essex Naturalist Trust and, over the years since, with the help of voluntary enthusiasts, great efforts have been made to restore some of the original wild and cultivated plants.

Warley Common has long been associated with military activity. Troops were there at the time of the War of Austrian Succession in 1742 and again in 1778 when there was fear of a French invasion as France supported the American colonies when they rebelled. 7,000 militiamen camped on the common and George III visited and reviewed the troops. A mock battle was also staged, which must have been an impressive sight. There were further musters late in the eighteenth century, but in 1805 permanent barracks were built for 2,000 cavalry. This was a useful location as it was just a day's march from Tilbury, where troops could embark for overseas postings.

After the end of the Napoleonic Wars the barracks were used less and less until, in 1842, they were bought by the East India Co. and used as a training centre for their troops before being sent abroad. Once again, soldiers stayed briefly before moving on.

The foundation stone of a county lunatic asylum was laid in 1851. This was said to be in Warley, although now it is hard to tell where the village ends and the town of Brentwood begins.

Warley also played its part during the First World War when Coombe Lodge, one of the large houses in the village, was used as a hospital for wounded soldiers. Although there were only eighty-three beds and an isolation tent in the garden, 2,140 of the wounded were tended there, although for most their stay must have been brief.

Warley Gap.

Today Warley is a quiet, picturesque village, although Eagle Way and the massive Ford office building standing on the site of the old barracks are reminders of a time when it rang to the march of military feet. For how many soldiers, one wonders, was this the last peaceful memory of England before being sent to the battlefields of Europe?

Pilgrims Hatch

Pilgrims Hatch falls within the borough of Brentwood. The word 'hatch' means gate and there may once have been a gate through which travellers passed when journeying towards Tilbury. The name was recorded in the fifteenth century, but it could have been in use earlier. Certainly some of the Canterbury pilgrims would have passed along the road leading towards Brentwood.

Notable in the village is the Black Horse. The whole building was gutted by fire in 1999, but has since been so carefully restored that it is hard to believe that it was almost completely destroyed.

At the edge of Pilgrims Hatch, on the Doddinghurst Road, is the Brentwood Centre, a sports and entertainments complex. Here the local football team has its ground and close by is the training school of the Essex Dog Display Team.

Shenfield

It is difficult for passers-by to know where the town of Brentwood ends and Shenfield officially begins. It already existed when the Domesday Book was being compiled; the name has Saxon origins and comes from Chenefield, which meant 'good lands'. The centre of the old village lay beside the Roman road, now the A1023, and must also have been used by pilgrims journeying to Brentwood and beyond. The Church of St Mary the Virgin lies a short way to the north of the main road with a popular primary school close by.

The Brentwood football ground at the Brentwood Centre.

Shen Place Almshouses.

Today Shenfield is an important railway junction. The station is close to a very busy shopping area where parking is often a major problem. The first buildings in Market Place were erected around 1907, although this is a strange name as there is no record of a market ever being held in the area and this is where Glantham's Farm once stood. Close by, the imposing Memorial Parish Hall was built in 1922 on land donated by the Courage family. With the exclusive Hutton Mount Estate just south of the main road, this is a thriving commuter area with good roads nearby and trains offering a frequent service into London. There is a direct line to Southend and Southminster, and trains also run to the north and east.

As well as the primary school, there is a large senior school with extensive playing fields and other sports facilities. The Courage Playing Fields have a popular play area and also a cricket pitch used by the Shenfield Cricket Club 3rd XI. The main cricket club also plays on land granted by the Courage brewing family. The badge of the club is a cockerel, the trademark of the brewery, and a cockerel also appears on the weathervane of the church, although this is more likely to be linked to St Peter.

Hutton

Situated to the east of Brentwood and very close to Shenfield is Hutton. It is known to have existed in the time of the compilation of the Domesday Book because, before the coming of the Normans, the land had been held by Goti, a freeman. Today, the village has a thriving residential population and supports several primary schools, namely: Long Ridings; St Joseph the Worker Roman Catholic School; All Saints Church of England School; Willowbrook, formerly Hutton County Primary School; and Brookfield. There is also Woodlands Preparatory School based at Hutton Manor. There are four public houses.

One sad story is recorded from the village. A police officer, Robert Babbrough, was given the job of escorting a criminal from Billericay Magistrates Court in November 1850. Somehow the fellow managed to overpower his captor and drowned him in a nearby pond. Robert was the first member of the Essex Constabulary to be killed whilst on duty.

Doddinghurst

Three miles to the north of Brentwood lies Doddinghurst. Mention of this village is also to be found in the Domesday Book, where it appears under the Anglo-Saxon name of Doddenhene. This meant 'the wood of Dudda', but the modern form of the name appears to have been in use by the thirteenth century. The church, All Saints, was restored in Victorian times but it still has its thirteenth-century doorway and a nave roof dating back to the fifteenth century.

This is a thriving village with, among other events, an annual donkey derby held in the park. The profits are divided between six local charities, the Doddinghurst Village Hall, the 1st Doddinghurst Scout Troop, Doddinghurst Olympic Football Club, Doddinghurst Church of England Junior School and also the infant and pre-schools. There is a row of shops and the Moat, the local public house

White's entry for the village in Victorian times describes it as being 'pleasant but straggling with a fruitful loam'. This is still an arable area, although there has been a substantial redevelopment since the 1950s.

Blackmore

The name of the village is thought to come from its extremely dark soil, originally being either 'Black Marsh' or 'Black Swamp'. There were a number of springs in the area and the land tended to be swampy. Now little of the dark earth remains.

Although not mentioned by name in the Domesday Book, two other manors in the parish are Fingrith and Copsheaves. The former can be traced to Saxon times when Edward the Confessor, ruled.

Blackmore Church seen through the lych-gate. The church incorporates part of the original priory.

Blackmore village pond.

Blackmore Priory dates back to 1155 when it was an Augustinian house dedicated to St Lawence. This unfortunate gentleman is believed to have been roasted on a gridiron in Rome – a most unpleasant form of martyrdom. The priory was founded by two chamberlains of the Queen, Adam de Sandford and Jordan. Later, in 1232, the canons of the priory were granted a fair by King Henry III. This was to be held at the time of the feast of St Lawrence, celebrated on 10 August. The fair continued to be held until late in the nineteenth century.

The fall of Blackmore Priory dates from the time of Henry VIII, although it was before the king's break with Rome. It was Cardinal Wolsey who decided that the priory would be useful for the founding of his colleges at Oxford and Ipswich in 1525. At that time, Blackmore was valued at approximately £85, but it only had a prior and three canons. In 1540 the king granted the priory to John Smyth, one of the royal auditors.

The new owner decided to demolish the priory in order to build his new mansion. Much of the monastic church was destroyed before the villagers obtained an injunction to stop further work, but to repair the damage he simply filled in the east wall with bricks. Most of the ancient nave has been incorporated into the nave and chancel of the newer building.

Henry VIII is not only remembered for his many wives, but also for his mistresses. One of these was Elizabeth Blount, daughter of Sir John Blount. She served Catherine of Aragon at court and her blonde beauty soon attracted the king. She became his mistress in 1518 and, before long, became pregnant. The illegitimate children of a monarch were usually born away from court, often in a religious house. Elizabeth was sent to Blackmore Priory where her son,

Henry Fitzroy, was born in June 1519. It is possible that Henry visited her there, although this is unknown. Certainly the king doted on his son and created him Duke of Richmond and Somerset. The boy died when he was just seventeen.

A Baptist church was built in the village in 1841 and in recent years there has been some housing development. Now further building has been stopped, apart from some rebuilding, as the centre of the village has been made a conservation area.

Kelvedon Hatch

Lying just north of Pilgrims Hatch and approximately four miles north of Brentwood, Kelvedon Hatch loses many of its residents each day as they commute to work. The village was mentioned in the Domesday Book as Kelenduna, Kalenduna and Kelvenduna, with the final name meaning 'speckled hill'. Until the middle of the twentieth century, agriculture and associated occupations were the main employers.

Kelvedon Hall came into the possession of John Wright in 1538 and it remained in his family until the early twentieth century, although the manor house had been rebuilt in the eighteenth century. Another important house in Kelvedon Hatch is Brizes, mentioned in Chapter 3.

A quiet-looking bungalow not far from the Ongar Road hides a secret. This was the entrance to a massive underground bunker, now known as 'the Secret Nuclear Bunker'. In 1952 the Cold War was at its height, nuclear war was feared and the government decided to take action by building a number of secret bunkers from which, in time of war, they could still function and make vital decisions for the safety of the country. This is the largest and deepest in Essex and is now open to the public. It has three underground storeys and a steep corridor leads down from the bungalow into a hidden world. This still has the damp, earthy smell found in underground shelters during the Second World War.

The entrance to the secret nuclear bunker, hidden beneath what is apparently a rural bungalow.

The villagers knew nothing of what was being constructed in their area, and military security was extremely tight. By the time it was finished, the bunker could have housed up to 600 personnel, including the Prime Minister. It had its own water supply, generators, radar room and even a scientists' room where the nuclear fallout patterns could be charted. Government ministers and the Prime Minister would have been based in the civilian operations room. Another important room was for the BBC. This would have been the centre from which all emergency broadcasts could be made, giving the surviving population information about what was happening.

The bunker was bought back by the original owner of the land in the 1990s when it was decommissioned. It has also been used as a location for films.

Mountnessing

The name 'Mountnessing' comes from the ancient family of Mountney or Monteny who owned the manor in the medieval period. The village existed at the time of the compilation of the Domesday Book, but at that time only a number of scattered farms were recorded. The Church of St Giles dates to at least the thirteenth century. Thoby Priory was founded in the area in around 1150 for Augustinian canons. The name came from the first prior, Tobias or Thoby. In the time of Henry VIII it ceased to be a religious house and was briefly granted to Cardinal Wolsey, who ordered its dissolution together with Blackmore Priory. His later fall from power led to the land passing into private hands.

The parish church is isolated from the village but it is known to date from Norman times. It is especially noted for its fine belfry.

Mountnessing windmill.

No visitor to Mountnessing can miss the beautiful windmill. It is a post mill built early in the nineteenth century and dominates the flat countryside around, rising above nearby buildings. It is now run by Essex County Council and has been well preserved. The mill is no longer used, but a steady stream of sightseers photograph the timber structure that stands on a circular brick base. It is close to the refurbished George and Dragon and is occasionally open to the public.

Ingatestone

Ingatestone and Fryerning combined in 1899 to form a civil parish, but they date back to Saxon times. The town grew up beside the Essex Great Road. The original name was 'Ging ad Petram', meaning 'settlement at the stone'. It is unusual to find stone in Essex. However, the one found at Ingatestone was deposited by glacial action which is rare so far south in Great Britain. It has been split into three separate parts, one of which is to be found by the west door of the church. The other two are either side of the narrow entrance to Fryerning Lane.

In the Domesday Book, Ingatestone was recorded as being in the Chelmsford Hundred. The land was held by Barking Abbey from around AD 950 and so it remained until the Dissolution of the Monasteries. At that time it came into the possession of Sir William Petre, a Devon lawyer who had become Secretary of State to Henry VIII. He was responsible for the building of a beautiful courtyard house, Ingatestone Hall, and also almshouses in Stock Lane. The house is still in the ownership of the Petre family.

Being on the Essex Great Road resulted in Ingatestone always being a town of passage and there have been royal visits in the past, although many were only fleeting. One notable visitor was Queen Elizabeth I, who stayed for several nights at Ingatestone Hall in 1561. This honour was very expensive for the host, but it is still remembered in the mural overlooking the market place where the monarch is shown in all her glory. Later, Charles I passed through as he travelled to Chelmsford to meet his mother-in-law, Marie de Medici. In the sad days of the Civil War, Roundheads pursued Cavaliers on their way to Colchester. In 1692 William and Mary paused for a meal in the town and Princess Charlotte also came through Ingatestone as she journeyed to meet her future husband, George III. On a less happy note, the unfortunate Princess Caroline's bier was drawn through the town in 1821 as her body was taken for burial in Brunswick.

By the eighteenth century, horse-drawn coaches regularly thundered along the Essex Great Road as they made their way towards Chelmsford, Colchester and the East Coast. However, the opening of the railway led to a decline in road transport and the town became quieter.

The dawn of the twentieth century saw new changes in the area. The town was close enough to London for commuters to feel that they could easily make the journey to work by train and return to the pleasant countryside each evening. This trend has continued and now there are many attractive new houses that blend well with the older ones to be found in the centre of town. In 1958 construction started on a long-awaited duel carriageway to bypass the town, and this is now the very busy A12 trunk road. The M25 can be reached in just ten minutes.

The centre of town is dominated by the Anglican Church of St Edmund and St Mary, with its impressive brick tower dating from around 1470. The nave is Norman but there may well have been an earlier Saxon church on the site, probably built of wood, but no traces survive.

Monuments to the Petre family can still be seen, including an alabaster tomb with effigies of Sir William Petre and his wife dating from 1572. There are also three other churches, which are Roman Catholic, Elim Penticostal and United Reformed.

Three schools are to be found in the town, an infants', junior and secondary. The junior school is a voluntary aided Church school with strong links to the parish church and the Anglo European School, mentioned in more detail in Chapter 6.

Ingrave and Herongate

The Ingrave Road goes south from Wilson's Corner in Brentwood, leading to the village of Ingrave and beyond. On the left stands the Church of St Nicholas. This impressive structure dates back to 1734 when it was built in brick on the orders of Lord Petre to the plans of an unknown architect. It was described by Professor Pevsner as 'the most remarkable eighteenth-century church in the country'. Its west tower, with its two octagonal turrets, is especially impressive. The church was built to replace a former parish church demolished when Lord Petre was having a new lawn laid at Thorndon Hall.

St Nicholas' Church at Ingrave.

Ingrave existed at the time of the Domesday Book and it lay in the Barnstable Hundred. Later pilgrims journeying south must have passed this small, rural community. Today the A128 is an extremely busy road leading from Brentwood to the A127. On the west side of the road, motorists may notice Hartswood, a municipal golf course, and further along the beautiful Thorndon Park, now one of the country parks surrounding Brentwood.

Herongate is a village also on the Ingrave Road. The famous Tyrrell family lived at Heron Hall and their name has been linked to a number of important historical events, although some are perhaps best forgotten. Walter Tirel (an early spelling of the name) was reputed to have been responsible for the death of William II. Sir John Tyrrell was in the personal retinue of Henry V and fought at Agincourt. He also served as an MP for Essex and acted as Speaker in three Parliaments. Rather less notable was the fact that his grandson, Sir James Tyrrell, was said to have been responsible for the murder of the Princes in the Tower and for this he was executed on Tower Hill in 1502. By the early years of the nineteenth century, what must once have been a very impressive house, Heron Hall, lay in ruins. However, the family name lives on in a memorial slab dedicated to Lady Alice Tyrrell, who died in 1422. This is in the Church of All Saints, East Horndon, a building that was almost entirely reconstructed by the generosity of the Tyrrell family.

6

Schools

There are many schools in Brentwood; private, state and also a number of Church schools. Several of them are unusually close to the centre of the town and any traveller approaching from the south along the Ingrave Road passes between two of the senior schools, Brentwood County High and Brentwood School. Both have interesting histories.

Brentwood School

Anthony Browne was the original founder of Brentwood School in 1557, which some believe was an act of contrition for the part he had played in the death of William Hunter. Whether this is true or not is open to debate, but for several centuries a massive elm tree grew close to the school's red-brick wall and this apparently flourished close to the place where the teenaged martyr was burnt at the stake. By the early years of the twentieth century, all that remained of the once mighty tree was a lifeless, decaying trunk. With the accession of King George VI in 1936, it was decided to remove this now dangerous stump and an oak tree was planted close by to take its place.

The Royal Licence to found the school was granted by the Roman Catholic Queen Mary just four months before her death. Over the years the school has faced high and low points, and this is only to be expected in an institution that has survived for so long. At first, education at the school was free for boys living within a three-mile radius who could read and write. In 1825 it was decided by the Charity Commissioners that only Latin and Greek scholars could receive a free education, and by 1852 the school had just forty-five boys on the register. However, 1881 saw everything change when Edward Bean became the headmaster. From that time on the school prospered; there were new classrooms built, a dormitory was erected over Old Big School and 1867-68 saw the construction of the chapel. The charismatic headmaster who brought about so many changes is still remembered in the name of the Bean Library. Since those times Brentwood School has become one of the most successful independent schools in the country, with over 1,000 pupils. Entrance to the school is by examination.

There have been many changes in recent years. The 1960s to the early '70s saw the school become a direct grant grammar school, but this scheme was abandoned in the mid-1970s. Throughout the centuries it had been a boys' school, but in 1974 it was decided to allow a limited number of girls into the Sixth Form. This was followed in 1986 by the opening of a purpose-built school for girls aged from eleven to eighteen. It was erected in the school grounds, beside Shenfield Road. At the time of writing, a new Sixth Form centre and auditorium is being constructed facing the Ingrave Road.

Brentwood School, Ingrave Road.

Brentwood Preparatory School moved into Middleton Hall, the former home of the Tasker family, in 1949. New buildings have since been added, but the old house maintains its majestic beauty. There is also a pre-preparatory school for ages three to seven.

Brentwood School has good examination results and its sporting achievements are notable. One Old Brentwoodian, Alex O'Connell, represented Great Britain for fencing in the Beijing Olympics and there have been many other successes in various sports.

Brentwood County High School

It was in the late 1870s that a private school for girls, started by Kate Bryan, opened in Queens Road. The building was known as Montpelier House. At that time there were a number of private schools for both boys and girls in the town. However, the majority did not survive long into the twentieth century. Kate Bryan's school was an exception, although it changed greatly over the years.

Brentwood County High School.

In 1913 the school was taken over by Essex County Council and became known as Brentwood County High School. Before long the Queens Road building was found to be unsuitable for the ever-growing number of students and in 1927 it moved to its present site beside Shenfield Common, close to the centre of town. School numbers continued to rise and by 1937 extensions were added so that 450 girls could attend.

The Second World War led to disruption for many children's education. Although only twenty-five miles from London, it was decided that Brentwood was a fairly safe town for the evacuation of youngsters from the capital. Like other schools in the area, Brentwood County High took in pupils from West Ham and Leytonstone with local children attending classes on Monday, Wednesday and Friday and the evacuees using the premises on Tuesday, Thursday and Saturday. Normal classes resumed in 1941.

It was in 1978 that the next major change occurred. Extensive building works had taken place and in that year the exclusive girls' grammar school became a mixed comprehensive with eleven-year-old boys being enrolled for the first time. Today, student numbers have increased to over 1,400 and teaching staff to more than ninety.

In 2004 the Brentwood County High became a specialist science, maths and computing school. This has led to extra funding in these areas, with excellent examination results following.

Brentwood County High School has now been a part of the town for well over 100 years. Although there have been many changes it remains a popular school, proud of its encouraging results in all fields of education.

St Thomas of Canterbury Church of England Junior School

It was in 1835 that a National School for girls was established to the south of Moore's Place close to St Thomas' Church. A National School for boys was set up in the old chapel. This was given a wooden floor, but apart from that the building was little changed. Reading, writing and arithmetic were taught, with the girls also learning needlework and religious education.

St Thomas' School plaque on the wall showing the martyrdom of St Thomas à Becket.

Both schools became overcrowded, so in 1869 it was decided to erect new schools in Love Lane, later to be known as Coptfold Road. The mixed infants' building was between the schools for the older boys and girls. Extensions were soon needed, especially after education became compulsory in 1880. This was an ever-growing problem in the following years, eased only when a new senior school for children over eleven opened in Sawyers Hall Lane in 1936. At that time, St Thomas' became a junior mixed school which, in 1968, moved to a new building in Sawyers Hall Lane. Coptfield House, the Centre for Essex County Council Social Services, now stands on the site of the old school buildings.

The school is now in two parts with infant and junior sections, both in Sawyers Hall Lane. As for all the Church schools, religious education is very important, but the curriculum covers all subjects. In the junior school there were twelve classrooms for the 310 children aged between seven and eleven enrolled in 2009. There is an information and communication technology (ICT) suite and also five rooms for small groups, a kiln room, a creative arts room and a children's kitchen. How different from those early days when the school was first started. Three music rooms are available for individual and small group lessons. Outside there is a large playing field, two playgrounds and an all-weather games pitch. Needless to say, St Thomas' School is very proud of the fact that it has been graded as 'Outstanding' in all its Ofsted inspections since 1998.

St Helen's Catholic Junior School

Roman Catholicism has always been strong in Brentwood, with many leading families involved in supporting both the Church and the schools. In 1861 the old St Helen's Chapel became a school. For many years the infants were to be found in Queens Road, opposite the cathedral. Then, in 1973, the junior school moved into purpose-built premises in Sawyers Hall Lane and the infants' school moved to the same area in 2009 when the old building was demolished.

St Helen's is a mixed voluntary aided Catholic school and serves the parishes of Brentwood, Warley, Ongar and Ingatestone. In all there are fifteen classrooms, ten in the main building and the others in a separate block. The hall is multi-purpose, being used for assembly, meals and school Masses. It is also equipped for PE. An ICT suite is available for up to thirty-two pupils at a time.

One facility of which the school is justifiably proud is a 20m indoor swimming pool, heated so that it can be used throughout the year. Other schools in the area are also able to benefit from using this pool.

Sawyers Hall College

The third school located in Sawyers Hall Lane is Sawyers Hall College. First opened in 1936, the two parts were known as Brentwood Senior Boys' and Girls' Schools. Later renaming took place when the school became Hedley Walter School, named after the Chairman of the Governors. In 1968 it was the first school in the area to become a comprehensive. The next major change occurred in 2003 when there was yet another name change as Hedley Walter was designated as a specialist science and technology school under the name of Sawyers Hall College.

St Helen's Roman Catholic School front door.

The school now caters for pupils aged from eleven to eighteen. Applicants from other schools may also be welcomed into the Sixth Form. A wide range of subjects is available for study throughout the school leading on to the General Certificate of Secondary Education (GCSE), Business and Technology Education Council (BTEC), National Vocational Qualifications (NVQ) and the National Diploma in Construction, which begins in 2009. Advanced Supplementary (AS) and Advanced (A) Level examinations are also available and a number of students go on to university or other institutions of further education.

Special events during the academic year made exciting reading in 2009. There was an educational visit to Gran Canaria for those students in Year Nine who had opted to study Spanish for GCSE. Three hours each morning were spent on Spanish lessons with the afternoons set aside for such activities as archery, biking, kayaking and windsailing. The biking even included time spent in a wilderness camp.

Technology is obviously important in a specialist college and recently students from Year Eight were able to participate in a special activity concerning the built environment. This involved teamwork as the pupils planned an eco town and a housing zone. Work was displayed on a wall showing the results of the study. There is now a new Diploma in Construction and the Built Environment for those in Year Ten and above.

Year Seven pupils also found out about bubonic plague and the effects of the Black Death with an actor visiting the school and vividly describing life in London during that terrible outbreak.

There were many other special events, but for Year Eleven students the celebrations at the end of GCSE examinations will undoubtedly stay with them for the rest of their lives. The De Rougemont Manor was the setting for the end of year prom, where school uniform was forgotten as students donned formal dress for this memorable evening.

Plans are now underway for closer links between Sawyers Hall College and Shenfield High School.

Brentwood College of Education

In 1962 Brentwood College of Education moved into Sawyers Hall Lane. For some years this was noted for the training of teachers. Later it became part of the Chelmer Institute of Higher Education and then a part of Anglia University. The building was also used for evening classes. In 1999 the college closed and the site has now been redeveloped for residential housing.

St Peter's Church of England Primary School

This is a voluntary aided school to be found in South Weald. In 1857 the then vicar of South Weald felt that there was a need to provide education for the children of the parish. The school was opposite the church, built on land donated by the vicar to designs by Teulon. The aim was 'to provide education according to the principals and practices of the Church of England'. The original building has now been demolished and a new one stands in Wigley Bush Lane.

St Peter's School.

The foundation stone for the new building was laid in 1956 and the first stage was ready for occupation the following year. Two more stages were opened in 1960. As the school has grown, further alterations and extensions have been necessary. At the end of the summer term in 2009, three new classrooms were finished, complete with solar energy panels to provide hot water. This latest development is connected to the main school by a walkway so that all eleven classrooms can be easily accessed without the need to venture outside. Each room is also equipped with toilets – how different from the days when the toilet block was usually placed well away from the main building, often on the far side of the playground.

The school has close links with the parish church. The vicar of St Peter's Church leads weekly worship and there is a service held in the church at the end of each term for the pupils and their families. Academic results are important and for two years running, Ofsted inspectors have graded the school as 'Outstanding', with perfect Standard Assessment Tests (SATS) results in English, maths and science.

An outdoor heated swimming pool is very popular with pupils and excellent results have been achieved in various competitions, both locally and at national level. Other sports include basketball, football, hockey, netball, cricket, rounders and rugby. Athletics and cross-country are also enjoyed.

St Mary's Church of England Voluntary Aided Primary School, Shenfield

This is a school with a long history. It has stood on its present site since 1865 and was built on land acquired by the parish rector, the Reverend Thomas Ferguson, through a trust. At first this was a school just for infants and girls and it had only two classrooms, with a house for the teacher. Within four years the school was extended to take in boys and a house for the master was added. Part of the original building remains in the junior school. Much has changed over the years but one important feature was added in 1893, when the school tower, complete with a clock, was erected. Sadly this happened the year after the death of the Reverend Thomas Ferguson, but a brass plate can still be seen inside the tower in memory of the rector of twenty-eight years whose foresight and hard work led to the establishment of the school. For many years the building was also used for local community and parish events, as it wasn't until 1922 that Shenfield Parish Hall was built.

There are still strong links between the school and the church. The building has undergone many changes over the years. A new infant unit was built in 1990 complete with three class bases and a central activity area. There are toilets and also a library. Further construction took place in 1997 with the building of a teaching block. This replaced some very old demountable classrooms. Even more recently there has been refurbishment of the reception and administration area which has improved security.

St Mary's has excellent academic results and is justifiably proud of the most recent Ofsted report where it was rated as an 'Outstanding' school. This is an extremely popular school, much sought after in the area.

The tower of St Mary's School, Shenfield.

Shenfield High School.

Shenfield High School

This comprehensive school is for eleven to eighteen-year-olds and has specialist status in business and enterprise, with maths and computing as secondary specialist areas. Since 2003 boys and girls have been taught in separate classes, although in form groups and socially the school is mixed. Extra-curricular activities are also mixed and it appears to work well for both the boys and girls.

The 1,500 pupils are drawn from a wide area covering Brentwood and Ongar. The buildings are on an extensive and very attractive twenty-acre green belt site. Sporting achievements are important and there is a large sports hall, indoor heated swimming pool and a gymnasium. The outdoor facilities include four football, two rugby and two hockey pitches. In the summer there are two cricket pitches, a running track and areas for other athletic sports. In 2004 the school received the Sports Council's much-coveted 'Goldmark' award. This has only been achieved by ten Essex schools.

Academic achievements are also important and very good results were obtained from a recent Ofsted inspection. Almost two-thirds of sixteen-year-olds gained five or more GCSE grades from A-C. This is well above the national average.

Whilst work in the classroom is important, so too are the extra-curricular activities. A wide variety of clubs can be enjoyed, and trips and visits have been many and varied. Overseas visits have included France, Germany, China, Poland and, in 2009, the World Challenge trip to Tanzania, the latter being for Year Twelve pupils. Other activities have included a canal trip, theatre visits and geography and biology field trips. This popular senior school is usually over-subscribed.

Above: Junction Road pupils, 1947. (By kind permission of Sylvia Kent)

Left: The new Holly Trees School.

Holly Trees Primary School

The original school in Junction Road opened in 1875, with a second opening by Essex County Council in 1904. At that time there was accommodation for 250 boys, girls and mixed infants. At first it was known as South Weald Council Mixed School but this was later changed. In 1936 the older children moved to the senior school and Junction Road became a junior school. The infant school was in Crescent Road. The name of the school changed to Holly Trees Primary School and in 2003 a brand new building was opened in Vaughan Williams Way. This was on the previous site of Warley Hospital's grounds.

Former students still recall the time when they went to the school carrying their gas masks in brown cardboard boxes. The building was close to the Warley Barracks and the railway so the risk of air raids was taken very seriously. There were shelters in the playground and lessons were often continued there during the raids.

Today, the school is a bright, happy place where children are encouraged to learn and relate to each other and the environment. When the new building was in the design stage, there was close involvement with the head teacher, members of the governing body, the County Council building project coordinator, the architect and the building contractors. With twelve classrooms, two halls (one equipped for PE), a library and a food hygiene room, the children are able to learn in pleasant surroundings and the results are encouraging.

St Martin's School

This is a co-educational, comprehensive foundation school. In the year 2000 it was designated by the Department for Educational Skills (DfES) as a National Beacon School of Excellence. In 2005 it became known as a high-performance school specialising in English, mathematics, technology, science, ICT and history. Dr Nigel Darby, the headmaster, takes a personal interest in the work of the pupils and he is involved in discussions with them on such matters as homework and their views on education in the school.

The school is situated in Hanging Hill Lane, Hutton, and pupils' ages range from eleven to nineteen. The land on which the school is built was called St Martin's Field, hence the name of the school. Although this is not a Church school, St Martin's Day is celebrated in a local church and afterwards gifts are distributed to elderly people in memory of the work of the saint.

A proud day in the history of St Martin's came in 2001 when Prince Andrew, the Duke of York, opened the largest part of the school's £6 million extension and upgrade. This included a sports hall, girls' changing rooms, an arts centre with ten studios, a library and resource centre, and a technology centre. A Sixth Form centre was created in 2003, with air-conditioned seminar rooms, a library, photographic studio, an information technology and study centre, a common room and a bistro.

With a maximum of twenty-four in each class, pupils have excellent learning conditions. Small groups make it possible to encourage active learning and results are impressive for SATs, GCSEs and A Levels. The religious studies department is especially proud of the fact that their pupils have achieved the best results in England for their subject.

Personal development is also very important. There is a wide range of activities available for sports and the arts. Lunchtime and after-school clubs are encouraged and there have been many trips and visits arranged both in England and abroad.

This is a happy school with many opportunities offered to students across the age and ability range.

The Endeavour School

The Ofsted report of 2006 was very complimentary towards the school. It is a mixed-sex day school for children with moderate learning difficulties. The aim is to develop the full potential of every pupil within an inclusive society. Self-sufficiency and independence are nurtured very effectively and the personal development of the pupils is excellent.

The Endeavour School.

The school is situated in Hogarth Avenue, within walking distance of the centre of the town. The website provides up-to-date information about the school, its aims, curriculum and activities and makes an additional form of communication with the community. At the Endeavour School all those involved with the children share the concerns of parents and guardians for the well-being of their charges. They say with confidence that the school has a happy, caring and industrious atmosphere.

Education is far more than the core curriculum. The school is also totally committed to developing the creative, physical, emotional and social life of the children in their care. The head teacher, Mick Southgate, is justly proud of the school and is always happy to show parents around, giving them a chance to experience the atmosphere.

The Anglo European School

The Anglo European School has been established since 1973 and was the first state school in Britain to offer the International Baccalaureate Diploma and also to become a specialist language college. Mrs Sarah Bain, the assistant head teacher, says:

> The AES is a very distinctive school with a clear focus on the development of internationalism and citizenship. The uniqueness of the school attracts students from a diverse range of cultures, which in turn further enriches the students' experiences. The school ethos of 'Think Globally, Act Locally' is central to its curriculum.

Many languages are available to students, including French, German, Spanish, Russian, Japanese, Italian, Chinese and Latin. In fact, the Anglo European School is one of the few schools in the country where all children are required to study two languages. There are plenty of opportunities for the young people to travel abroad as part of the school's visits programme, often on exchanges.

This is a self-governing, co-educational school with just over 1,300 pupils of mixed ability aged between eleven and nineteen. It is located in Ingatestone, with ample bus and train links covering the area. Unusually, the Anglo European School has two head teachers, Mrs Jill Martin and Mr David Barrs. The school aims to provide a high quality of education, enriched by a strong European and international dimension

An extra-curricular programme plays a very important part in the life of the school. Sporting activities are encouraged at all levels. Cricket, netball, rugby and hockey are played and there is an enthusiastically supported annual Sports Day which is held at the Melbourne Athletics Stadium in Chelmsford. The music department encourages a jazz band, a woodwind group, choirs and ensembles. Other activities include a school play and involvement in the UK Mathematics Challenge. The Anglo European School plays a unique part in the educational life of the area and is committed to the all-round development of its young citizens.

Adult Education

There are many opportunities for Brentwood residents to follow courses in a wide variety of subjects. These classes are run by Essex County Council. Bishops Hill is a popular venue. Once a residential school, this building, especially its beautiful hall, lends itself to educational needs.

Bishops Hill Further Education Centre hall.

The Warley Centre is also much used, as are a number of local schools. Saturday workshops are popular and include arts and crafts, music, gardening, IT, first aid and many other subjects to fire the imagination. Classes for a number of qualification examinations are also available.

The Future

Unfortunately it is impossible to include all the local schools in this chapter. Each one is unique and makes its own contribution to education in Brentwood. The young people of any town are its future and here the local schools can be justly proud of their achievements.

7

The Brentwood Tales

Geoffrey Chaucer informs us that when pilgrims made their way to Canterbury, they told each other tales when they paused to rest. Travellers with little other evening entertainment must have eagerly exchanged information about themselves and the places from which they had come. Today our town is full of interesting people, each with a story to tell, and so we now come to our very own Brentwood Tales.

The Mayor's Tale
Councillor Dudley Payne, Mayor of Brentwood 2008-2009

I was born in Sussex Road, close to Warley Hospital, and went to school locally. Apart from six brief months away, I have always lived in Brentwood. It was almost by chance that I first became a local councillor. A friend who had served in Hutton North Ward was moving away and he suggested that I might like to seek election in his place. That was in 2000, the year of the new millennium. One-third of the Council stands for re-election each year, except in the fourth year, so I have faced several elections since then.

Before becoming Mayor you are invited to stand for election as Deputy Mayor. This is usually done on a seniority basis, depending on how long you have served on the Council. However, not everyone is willing or able to stand and it doesn't automatically mean that a Deputy Mayor will take over as Mayor, even though this usually happens. The Deputy Mayor is proposed and seconded and then elected by his or her peers in the Council chamber. The same process is followed before the new Mayor takes office

After a year as Deputy Mayor, my nomination form was signed in April 2008 and I became Mayor in May of that year. It was then that I realised that, for the next twelve months, my life would be in someone else's hands. At that moment, I became the official representative of the borough.

Although I remained a councillor, the life of the Mayor is completely different. As a local councillor you concentrate mainly on ward issues and if you become chairman of a committee, your horizons widen. However, they become much wider for the Mayor. At that point you are Chairman of the Council and run the Council meetings. In fact, before we had a Mayor the office was known as Chairman of the Council.

It is difficult to choose one event during my year as Mayor that stands out above all the rest, because everything was equally significant in its own way, whether it was the garden party at Buckingham Palace or a visit to a group of Brownies who were fundraising for breast cancer.

Above left: The Mayor of Brentwood, Councillor Dudley Payne.

Above right: Mayor Dudley Payne, John Fryer and Doreen Butterman, Chairman of Brentwood Museum Society, outside the Town Hall unveiling engravings showing the history of Brentwood.

They were all important and memorable to the people concerned and also to me. As Mayor, there are very few functions you attend just for yourself. You are there as the representative of the borough and the representative of the Queen at borough level.

Of course, the garden party at Buckingham Palace was a very special event. It took place on a Tuesday in July and fortunately the weather was fine, because this is an outdoor event. The next day it rained. It was a very memorable experience, being so close to the Queen and Prince Philip. When they came to walk amongst us, they split up with the Prince going one way and the Queen the other. Her Majesty came our way. She is quite tiny, but that is hardly noticed as she has such a tremendous presence.

One thing that really struck me during my year as Mayor was how active the voluntary sector is in the Brentwood community. Without the support these volunteers give, it would be impossible to sustain many of the services that are offered. Those helpers cover the complete age range, with many of the most enthusiastic being young people. Unfortunately, this age group often misses out on the credit it deserves. I have met hundreds of children who are very helpful and respectful.

It is impossible to remember every person who I met during my very special year. However, they remember me! When I attended a Scout jamboree I met a large contingent from Brentwood. One young man reminded me that I had presented prizes at his school. I also presented prizes at the Hermitage. Another reminded me that I had previously presented prizes at a function called 'Fire Break'. That was for children who were having difficulty at school and were taken away for a week and given basic training in fire-fighting skills and teamwork. That week had changed his attitude towards life and given him new confidence and he wanted to tell me, as Mayor, what a difference it had made.

The life of the Mayor is made easy because of an excellent support team. The Deputy Mayor has to drive himself, but the Mayor has five different drivers, all of whom are extremely competent. Sarah Furlong is the Mayor's secretary and she is very efficient and well organised. When a visit involves a speech, she finds out first what is needed and how long it should be. When you are addressing an organization, you need to be able to give them a boost.

Each year the Mayor supports certain local charities and he raises as much money as possible throughout his year in office. These have to be selected carefully so that the same charity is not chosen year after year. I chose the Ingrave Community Centre on the East Ham Estate, which has fallen into disrepair, where local residents formed a charity to raise money for rebuilding. I was very keen to help as my own wedding reception was held there a number of years ago. My other charity was the Claire-Louise Ferris Trust Fund. Claire-Louise was in her early twenties when she died in a car accident. She had founded a dance school at Kelvedon Hatch and her family has set up the fund to see that her work carries on. One event that is always a good fundraiser is the Mayor's Charity Challenge, part of the annual Town Centre Cycle Races.

It has been a great honour to represent Brentwood as Mayor and memories of my very special year will remain with me for the rest of my life.

The Archer's Tale
Ian Moriai, member of Holdens Archers

I originally come from North Kensington and lived in a house off the Portobello Road. After marriage and a number of moves in London, we lived in Battersea. At that time I worked for a shipping company in the City. Being married with four young children we were rapidly running out of space in our small house. A number of my colleagues at that time lived in Essex, travelling to and from Liverpool Street. This prompted us to look in this direction and we finally found a suitable place in Brentwood. We moved here in 1970 and have remained ever since.

My interest in archery came about almost by chance. The local engineering company I worked for after leaving the City went into liquidation and I became redundant. I was fortunate that I was offered a job in a stationery shop in the High Street. The owner of the shop often talked about archery and I learned that he was in fact Chairman of Holdens Archers, a local archery club. I played a lot of football and cricket in my time and have dabbled in many other sports, but apart from Robin Hood and Agincourt I didn't know of the existence of the sport. I took an initial course of lessons and decided that archery was for me, so I joined the club. That was fifteen years ago and I have been shooting with them ever since. The membership of the club varies. We have been up to fifty, but at the moment the number is around thirty.

We meet at the Society of Old Brentwoods' sports field for outdoor shooting and in the winter on Wednesday evenings we move to Keys Hall, Warley. This is a target archery club that shoots at the traditional, coloured circular target with a gold centre.

Ian Moriai, a keen archer.

The majority of members use a recurve bow, which is a high-tech version of the traditional longbow, although this bears little resemblance to the bows of old. Now they are often made of nano-carbon fibre, laminated hybrid foam and other modern materials, with all sorts of attachments. A few members still persist with the wooden longbow – the old bent stick.

For a beginner, the initial outlay could be a few hundred pounds. For the really serious archer, this could be £2,000 or £3,000. Because archery is a minority sport, the number of specialist equipment shops is limited. The nearest one to Brentwood is in Braintree. It is advisable to visit such a shop for initial equipment as it is most important that the draw weight of the bow is suitable for the archer, the weight being the amount of effort needed to draw the bow back fully before releasing the arrow. Each specialist shop operates a comprehensive mail order service.

In Great Britain, the sport is governed by the Grand National Archery Association which, in turn, is affiliated to the International Archery Federation. The club is affiliated to the Essex County Archery Association and, at the present time, there are something like sixty clubs in the Essex and Suffolk area, so anyone interested is never far from a club.

There are many levels of competition ranging from Olympic, international and county to local clubs. The sport is open to all, including people with most types of disability. I have found archery to be a bit of a personal thing. When you're shooting you're on your own; no one can help you. If you're hitting the centre of the target you're on top of the world. If you're not shooting well and it's the beginning of the shoot and you've got another three or four hours to go before the end, it can be very, very character building!

Being an old sport, archery has many written and unwritten rules regarding safety, procedure, etiquette, behaviour and dress. Most of it is just common sense. It is a good hobby and an excellent way of passing time outdoors. I used to shoot four times a week but have cut back recently.

A quiz night organised by the Stroke Club and supported by Holdens Archers.

The club runs a regular archery activity course at a local school where we instruct youngsters in the basics of archery; we also run 'Come and Try' events at local fêtes.

The club does not have a great social side. The main pleasure is meeting other members regularly on the field. In the past we ran barn dances and race nights. These have now been replaced by quiz nights, which are well attended and are supported by the Stroke Club. We, in turn, support their functions.

One of our main events of the year is our charity shoot in aid of leukaemia research. This is open to any interested archer from any club and 2009 will be the twenty-sixth time the event has been held. In that time, nearly £7,000 has been raised for this cause.

I have thoroughly enjoyed the sport and the company. It has been an important part of my life for the past fifteen years.

The Traveller's Tale
David Clamp, VSO

Although I wasn't born in Brentwood I always consider it my home because it is where I grew up. From an early age I loved exploring and maps fascinated me. In fact, they have always played a large part in my life. I used to draw huge maps with my other friends from Brentwood School and, when I was a little older, the school gave me the chance to go off and explore strange new areas. These included the Lake District, the Isle of Arran in Scotland and finally Norway, where I was able to scale some of the ice fields.

Mike Blooman, one of the teachers at the school, planned an expedition to the Himalayas. I left school and had a year out before university to earn enough money to pay for the trip. Until that time I had never travelled beyond Europe but, at the end of my gap year, I joined a small group of my former classmates and we set off to journey to India and through Nepal. It was absolutely fascinating and having such an erudite teacher and guide with us meant that the trip became a formative experience for me. We trekked 200 miles from Kathmandu all the way up to Everest Base Camp and even higher than that – in fact, as high as you can go without the aid of oxygen, which is two-thirds of the way up the flanks of Mount Everest. That was quite a step for three seventeen-year-olds from Brentwood.

That trip set me off on a particular course in my life. Since then I've spent most of my adult life working for Voluntary Service Overseas (VSO), an organization that sends skilled people to developing countries where those skills are in short supply. I started off as a volunteer teacher trainer in the rural south of China, in Guangxi Province. I worked at a teacher training college where I was helping eighteen to twenty-one-year olds to become English teachers. My aim was to put a little more imagination into their teaching, so they were able to vary the traditional way of learning using the blackboard that they were used to.

Coming back home, my taste for adventure had not abated and I joined the staff of VSO in London. Since then I've had the most incredible time. I spent six years in the Gambia, West Africa, first running education programmes and later as the Country Director taking responsibility for all our programmes in the country. I worked with over 100 volunteers from ten different countries who were employed in the fields of education, health, rural development and supporting disabled people in the Gambia.

David Clamp, planning to travel.

Now I'm back in London and managing VSO's security in the forty-four countries where we work. In the last year I've been on the road again, in Pakistan, Nigeria, India and Papua New Guinea. My next stop is Sierra Leone.

I am now relating this tale from the same house in Brentwood where I grew up. It has been a long journey, and I have met many fascinating people and seen incredible sights, but I have always come back here to the town where I first gained my love of travel and the urge to see the world.

The Journalist's Tale
Sylvia Kent, freelance writer

I came to Brentwood in 1966 when I married Peter. We lived in Herongate, before six years later moving to Hartswood Road, Brentwood. My husband had grown up in the town and his father was a local policeman, often to be seen patrolling the High Street. His mother was a nurse at Highwood Hospital.

Over the years I worked as a freelance secretary for many organizations in and around the town. This gave me the chance to be at home whenever our two daughters were not at school.

I have always loved reading and writing and this eventually led me into journalism. I suppose this really started when I was a Brownie and won my Writer's Badge. Amazingly, this was presented by Enid Blyton at the Central Methodist Hall in Westminster. To me she seemed to be very old, but she was only in her mid-fifties!

Writing started as a hobby. I worked for Hansard in Westminster from 1979 until 2005 and that meant that I mixed with many writers, journalists and politicians. This undoubtedly influenced me because we were using language and words, and accuracy was vital. I joined the University of the Third Age and there I met a wonderful journalist called Mary Bourne. She had previously worked for *Punch* and the *Telegraph*. We got on very well and I discovered that she ran the U3A writing group. She encouraged me to write about one of my hobbies which, at that time, was winemaking. I had just won the Essex Wine Federation Mead Competition and she suggested that I should write an article on making a gallon of mead. This I did and then she said, 'Send it off to a magazine'. I was thrilled, some time later, to receive a cheque. Then a second article was accepted, this time by *The Lady*.

Next I approached a local newspaper, offering to write a column for them. They agreed that I could send in two features on winemaking. Following that, I wrote a column every week for a year. During this time I joined the Brentwood Writers' Circle. That was useful as some of the speakers were most helpful. I am now Vice President of this extremely active society, the oldest in Essex.

By that time I had really caught the writing bug and I was sending off other work. At the same time I began looking at local history. The editor of the *Weekly News* suggested that I should write a weekly historical column. That was sixteen years ago and it is something I am still doing. In fact, I have gone into other genres as well; local history, people and places, clubs and associations, and gardening. Photographs are very important to illustrate articles and I now have a large library of images taken from the time I started writing.

Together with my local column I have also worked for many magazines, and have contributed to the *Daily Telegraph*, the *Daily Mail* and other 'dailies'. Some of my celebrity interviews came

Sylvia Kent, a freelance journalist. (By kind permission of Sylvia Kent)

The Yorkshire Grey, a well-known former public house in the High Street, *c.* 1900. This comes from Sylvia Kent's collection of early photographs of Brentwood. (By kind permission of Sylvia Kent)

from my work at Westminster and have included Betty Boothroyd, the former Speaker of the House of Commons, and MP Anne Widdecombe. There have also been people from the world of show business, including television celebrities, actors and Olympic athletes.

As a writer I find it very useful to enter competitions and have won five international writing awards. Winning a competition is excellent for a writer's reputation. I was Overseas Liaison Officer for the Society of Women Writers & Journalists for eight years and I am now their Press Officer and Archivist. Also, I have contributed to national and local radio, helped with the making of historical films and enjoy being a patron of the Essex Book Festival.

To me, Brentwood is a fascinating town. We have a number of fine local historians, and I have strong links with the library and also the Essex Record Office. Both have helped with my local history books, including two on Brentwood.

The Parliamentarian's Tale
Eric Pickles, Member of Parliament for Brentwood and Ongar
Based on an interview with Frances Clamp

I was born in Keighley, West Yorkshire, where my father ran a general store. I first became interested in politics when I was sixteen years old. My great-grandfather had helped to found the Independent Labour Party and my family were activists who all voted Labour. At that time, I too was on the left of politics. Then the Soviet Union, as it was then called, invaded Czechoslovakia. I felt I wanted to protest about this destruction of democracy, and decided the best thing I could do would be to join the Conservative Party. I spent the next few years attending Young Conservative discotheques, coffee mornings and cheese and wine gatherings until eventually the Soviet system was brought down!

I thoroughly enjoyed being a Young Conservative and eventually became Chairman, then Regional Chairman and finally National Chairman of the Youth Association.

I was elected as a Conservative councillor and became leader of Bradford Metropolitan Authority, the fourth largest Council in the country with a budget of close to £1 billion. At the time the Council had sub-committees with larger budgets than the whole of Brentwood Borough Council. Usually you would be in your mid-fifties to take on a job like that, but I was in my mid-thirties and was thinking about what to do next. Should I leave politics or try for Parliament? I was undecided.

At that point I went to a Spring Conference at Scarborough. A hand with a vice-like grip grabbed me by the elbow and I looked round. It was Margaret Thatcher.

'Come with me,' she said.

I was virtually frog-marched across the room to the Vice Chairman of the Party.

'Mr Pickles would very much like to be a Member of Parliament and I'd be grateful if you would interview him,' Mrs Thatcher announced.

I received an application form, filled it in and went off to a weekend residential course to find out what I was letting myself in for. After that I was on my own and started applying for various seats, including Brentwood, and was offered several interviews. When I came to Brentwood I discovered 316 other people had also applied to stand as the Member of Parliament. Fortunately I was selected. I moved to the town which I now consider my home.

I have found Brentwood to be a kind town with many local people keen to put something back into their community. Events like the Church flower festivals and many other occasions I am invited to attend show this involvement. The individual villages also have great support when they organise events.

I try to be available in Brentwood on Fridays and usually on Saturdays and Sundays as well so I can visit constituents and events taking place over the weekend. I leave for my Parliamentary

Eric Pickles MP.

Above left: Medieval shop buildings in the High Street.

Above right: The old Post Office (1891-1939) and St Thomas' Church. (By kind permission of Sylvia Kent)

work either very late at night or early the next morning depending on how early the first meeting of the day has been scheduled.

The political situation is likely to change very rapidly. No two days are ever the same. People sometimes believe that everything finishes at ten o'clock, but taking part in debates in the chamber is only a very tiny part of the job. I arrived home this morning at 12.15 a.m. and by 7.30 a.m. was at a meeting with Sixth Formers for one of my regular breakfast briefings. I enjoy meeting young people from Brentwood and Ongar; once they become engaged in debate, I find I often do not have to say very much because the conversation naturally flows.

I see Brentwood as a town of passage. It was a pilgrims' town and it was also a coaching town. You can still see some of the old coaching inns. Apart from that it was also a market town. Now new development is due to take place in William Hunter Way and this will change the nature of the town from a linear layout to a conventional square, so I believe the physical nature of Brentwood is going to change. The question is, will it actually change the nature of the town itself? I think that the merging of the pavement with the road in Crown Street is, in many ways, an allegory of what the town wants to achieve. The pace of traffic will slow and it will become a little more pedestrian friendly. Although not preventing cars from driving through the town centre, it should result in us showing more respect for each others' space. If we get rid of much of the clutter and bollards in the High Street, I think we will make sure that the nature of the town becomes much more reflective of the people who live here. The High Street will change and the new development will come. This is controversial, but if you look through the archives you can see that quite a number of past developments have also been very controversial. This includes changing the Town Hall and even the introduction of the railways.

When I look at the various communities and villages they each have a distinctly different pace. People may come originally for work or children's education, but then they tend to stay. There are so many things to keep the community going and I feel privileged to represent the town in Parliament. I have now spent much of my adult life in the area and it is the place I think of as home.

The Golfer's Tale
Michael Sorenti, member of the European Senior Masters' Tournament team

I came to Brentwood in 1971, after living for a while in Seven Kings. I started playing golf around fifty-five years ago, after first being an enthusiastic cricketer. I had played for the Essex Young Amateurs for a while, but it was too far to travel regularly to Colchester where they were based. For a time I played locally at Hole End and the South East Essex Club, but then someone introduced me to golf. After that there was no looking back. I had caught the golf bug. I joined Maylands Golf Club in 1954, even before we moved to Brentwood, but since 1980 I have been a member of Thorndon Park.

I have played in many competitions over the years, but the real highlight of my golfing career was playing for the United Kingdom in the European Senior Masters' Tournament. The first time was in Luxembourg and we actually won the title. That was in 2007 and the following year we played in Holland and came second in one group and third in another. A trophy was awarded at the end. Wives came too and my wife, Angela, thought the whole thing was fantastic. All the wives mingled very well and in Luxembourg in particular, two ladies from the Luxembourg Golf Club took the ladies around the city and entertained them to lunch. We paid for our own accommodation but our entry fee was covered by the Association. There were twenty-two teams taking part when we went to Luxembourg and also to Holland.

Michael Sorenti, a golfer in action.

This year the Senior Masters' Tournament will be in Reykjavik in Iceland. Possibly this may cut back the numbers who compete as the fare is extremely expensive. To play for the UK Seniors you must have a handicap of eight or less. My lowest handicap was three. There is a summer meeting for UK Seniors where there are various age groups. They start at fifty-five and then go to sixty, sixty-five, seventy and over seventy.

I have played for both my Brentwood clubs for the Thornton Cup. This was started by someone from British Rail who managed to get together some golf clubs that were associated with stations in and around London and Essex. This became a league. I first played in the competition in 1975 when I had a four-stroke handicap. I have also been successful in winning a number of local club cups over the years. A cup is usually held for a year, but you keep a replica. While I was working I was at one time a member of United Kingdom Provision Exchange Golf Society. This covers six different areas across the country. I captained the Society in around 1981 and there was a team of eight.

In the past golf equipment was extremely expensive, but now it has become quite reasonable. You can pick up a good set of golf clubs for £350. That is for the irons and you also need some woods. A good, complete set probably costs around £500 or £550. Club heads are now metal and shafts are often made of graphite. To me this is great because clubs now are much lighter and, as you get older, they seem easier to use. To hit the ball a long way you need maximum club head speed when you connect with the ball and this is helped by lighter equipment. You certainly don't need new clubs every year, as manufacturers imply, although after six or seven years the shafts do wear and they lose some of their elasticity. Professionals or top amateurs may need to change them more frequently, but not the average player. Of course, most top professionals would be provided with their clubs by sponsors. Now golf balls are also being changed so they can go 20 or 30yds further after being hit with the same club.

Originally, balls were filled with feathers but now they are made of a composition filling. Some people feel that progress has gone too far because some professional golfers can hit a ball 350yds off the tee. Perhaps the courses themselves could be made more difficult by introducing further hazards or sloping the greens. There are all sorts of ways of doing this with the use of new technology and this may be the way golfing should go in the future. A couple of years ago a metal club was introduced which had a face that had a springing effect when it hit the ball. This has now been prohibited.

Brentwood has some excellent golf clubs, both public and private, and it is a game that can be enjoyed at all levels.

The Musician's Tale
Ann Elderton, music teacher, violinist and pianist

My childhood was spent in Ingatestone. When my father played the piano I tried to copy him and that is where my interest in music really started. Piano lessons followed when I was seven, but when I was eleven I became fascinated with the violin. Before long I was at the same standard as for the piano.

When I was about fourteen, I joined my first orchestra. It met at King Edward's Grammar School in Chelmsford. Someone there asked if I would like to go along to the Essex Symphony

Ann Elderton, musician.

Orchestra, which I did, and I also had an audition for the Essex Youth Orchestra. For a couple of years I played in the 2nd Youth Orchestra before joining the 1st Orchestra.

Teaching started while I was still at school and continued after I left and went to study at the Royal Academy of Music, following an audition. Luckily I could still get home at weekends and that way I earned some pocket money by teaching. Although I went to the academy at first to study as a pianist, in the back of my mind I knew that I really wanted to be a strings teacher. Once I had passed my piano diploma, I changed to study for my violin diploma. While there Lees Hawarth, the head of music at Hedley Walter School, invited me to teach at their music school on Saturday mornings.

After finishing training I moved to Brentwood in 1970 and started building up my private teaching practice, as well as doing peripatetic work in local schools. I was also playing in various orchestras in and around Essex. In the early days of the Brentwood Philharmonic, I was the leader of the orchestra.

Over the years I have taught violin in most of the schools in Brentwood, both primary and senior. I must admit I prefer teaching the younger children. St Thomas of Canterbury is where I have stayed for the longest time, thirty-seven years in total.

Since 1990 my passion has become providing Brentwood's young musicians with the opportunity to experience the delights and camaraderie of playing together in orchestras. The Brentwood Youth Orchestra began in the late 1970s and a number of my pupils joined. I felt it would be advantageous to have a string orchestra for younger children to feed the Youth Orchestra so, in 1990, I started the Brentwood Junior String Orchestra. I am still the conductor and it has gone from strength to strength. In the late 1990s my daughter, Sarah, and I founded the Brentwood Beginners' Strings because there were so many young players who wanted to join the BJSO. They could start at a very elementary level and learn how to play together, ready to move into the Junior Strings later.

The Phoenix FM Station.

By the mid-1990s, after some problems, the numbers in the Youth Orchestra had dropped considerably. It needed a new look so I joined Elspeth Bingley, Youth Arts Co-ordinator for the Council of the time, and the then conductor of the orchestra, Antoine Mitchell, to rescue the orchestra. In September 2000 it reformed as the Phoenix Youth Orchestra, which rehearses weekly during term time and gradually the numbers have recovered. The ages range from Year Eight upwards and most stay until they go on to further education.

Although I am a strings specialist, I realised that there was nothing for wind players so I contacted wind teachers in the area. In January 2003 a wind band was started. It is known as the Phoenix Wind Band. This has a wider age range, from eight to fifteen. Between forty and fifty members meet once a month for a couple of hours and they also have workshops.

In September 2003 I launched a training orchestra for those of secondary age, often late starters who are not yet advanced enough for the Youth Orchestra. This is known as Phoenix Flames. The reason for forming a separate group was that those in senior school didn't mix well with the younger children. They stay in Flames until they reach Grade Five or Six. Flames is a full orchestra with strings and wind, and in 2009 it became larger than the Youth Orchestra! (Brentwood Junior Strings will have around thirty members and the Beginners' Strings nearly forty.) Judith Underwood, a flautist, has also recently started a flute choir.

Recently it was decided to join the six orchestras together under the umbrella name of Brentwood Orchestra for Young Musicians. All the orchestras perform regularly and one or other can often be seen at various public functions such as the Strawberry Fair and the Christmas lighting-up of Brentwood. In September 1993, BJSO was the first to perform at the dedication ceremony in the new, and then unfinished, Brentwood Theatre. At the opening of the new Phoenix Radio studio, a number of orchestra members performed and since then they have been featured on the music programme.

Music for young people in Brentwood is alive and thriving. Let's hope that the enthusiasm they have developed here will continue and grow for the rest of their lives.

8

Recreation

Brentwood is a busy town and there are many forms of recreation available to residents. Sports facilities and health centres abound and individual sports are well catered for. Clubs cover all interests, ranging from flower arranging to the local historical society. The town has its own theatre, small but well supported, and there are groups for drama, the visual arts, photography and painting. There are also orchestras, choirs and operatic societies, all ready to give their time to entertain the local population.

Brentwood Arts Council

The Arts Council is a registered charity organised by a committee and it plays a vital role in the community. About fifty organisations are affiliated to the Council with a very wide range of interests, including music in all its forms, drama, the visual arts, the written word and also Brentwood's heritage. The Arts Council distributes grants to help with the work of the various groups and co-ordinate their activities, thus avoiding clashes when special events are planned. An anti-clash diary is available to reduce the likelihood of double dating

The Council came into existence in 1970 with Col. Robert Tong as President. Right from the start, members of Brentwood Urban District Council Town Centre Development Committee were involved and there is continuing financial support from Brentwood Borough Council. At first, various public events were organised and concerts attracted such well-known names as Julian Lloyd Webber, Jake Thackeray and Humphrey Littleton. Later, home-grown entertainment became important. The opening of the Brentwood Centre was celebrated with the Essex Youth Orchestra performing with others at a special gala concert.

The Brentwood Arts Council, now known by the shorter title of Brentwood Arts, continues to do sterling work for the artistic life of the town with the current President being Lord Petre.

Old House, the Hermitage Gallery and the Hermit Club

Old House is a creeper-covered building that has been used for a number of years as an arts and community centre. Many local organisations have used it for their meetings and there is a comfortable café available.

The Hermitage, Shenfield Road.

The building has a long and interesting history and it is known to have existed since at least 1748. In the early years of the nineteenth century it was inherited by Mrs Harriet Manby on the death of her husband. In those days it had a paddock, pleasure ground and field, but open spaces so close to the High Street have long since disappeared. The land is now used for car parking and a towering telephone exchange also occupies part of the site. At one time it was the Red Lion Inn. It was later the home of the well-known Rist family who traded in the High Street, and after this it was a boarding house for Brentwood School.

The Hermitage Gallery, close to Old House, is used for youth arts and as a media studio, giving young artists a place to display their work. The Hermit Club, also in Shenfield Road, is a very popular venue for live music and caters for a wide age range. Rock, jazz, the blues and folk music may all be enjoyed at this centre.

The Brentwood Centre

The Brentwood Centre first opened its doors in 1988 and since then it has played an important part in many aspects of the life of the town. Entertainment, sports and leisure activities all are to be found at this important complex.

The International Hall can seat up to 2,000, but it is a multi-functional facility and can be used for many purposes. A number of internationally famous entertainers have come to the centre, normally playing to packed audiences. The hall also has twelve badminton courts

The Brentwood Centre.

and can be adapted to the needs of many other sporting activities. In fact, a whole range of sports are available including football, table tennis, aerobics and various other activities, including yoga. There is also a health suite, a high-tech fitness centre, beauty clinic, therapy rooms, squash courts and a crèche for parents involved in the many activities offered at the centre.

The playing fields around the main building host a variety of outdoor activities, including football, rounders, tennis and netball on floodlit courts. There are also exhibitions, fireworks displays and model aircraft flying. The Essex Dog Training Centre is to be found to the north of the site.

The Brentwood Theatre

The Brentwood Theatre Trust was formed in 1978. Years of campaigning followed as attempts were made to raise funds to start the building. At that time Brentwood was the largest town in England without a dedicated theatre space. Finally the hard work paid off. In 1993 the theatre was able to open its doors to the public. The site is good, located in Shenfield Road behind the Hermitage and close to Wilson's Corner.

This is very much a community theatre with a large team of volunteers giving their time to help both in front of house and backstage. The majority of productions are by amateur companies who arrange their rehearsals in local halls, provide costumes and build scenery.

The Brentwood Theatre.

Over forty separate groups use the theatre for their productions and more than 15,000 attend the shows over the year. In fact, those wishing to use the theatre are often surprised to discover that it is likely to be fully booked twelve months in advance.

For a number of years the theatre existed without proper dressing rooms. The Friends of Brentwood Theatre set about fundraising and the work has finally been completed Not only are there now proper dressing rooms but also a new office, washroom, a galley kitchen and a multi-use space with full mirrors that can be used as a dance studio, a rehearsal area or even as a forty-seat studio theatre.

Swimming

From the 1930s the town boasted a fine outdoor swimming pool. This was located in North Road, not far from the centre of the town. The site had previously been known as Debtor's Field. Beside the pool was a paved area, popular with sunbathers, and also a grass verge often used by picnickers. However, as years passed, needs changed. When the Brentwood Centre was built it incorporated two excellent indoor swimming pools and the old pool was no longer required. For a time, part of the site became a children's recreation area until the land was acquired for the building of a new Sainsbury's superstore. In 2009 new equipment arrived and the children once more have their own play area where the swimming pool of the 1930s was once to be found.

There are many activities in the pools. Fitness swimming is encouraged when the main pool is divided into various lanes, two for slow swimmers, two for those reaching medium speeds and two for those who are fast. This means that all swimmers can move at a speed that suits them, without impeding the progress of others. Casual swimming is when the pool is open to the general public, but one fast and one slow lane remain for those who prefer to use them.

The 'Water Workout' involves exercise to music in the shallow end of the main pool, with a qualified instructor in charge. A popular water aerobics class is held on a Wednesday morning, while 'Splashtime' is a fun session when inflatables and floats are used in both pools. There is also an 'adults only' time specifically for those over the age of sixteen. 'Aquacess' is held on Sundays for swimmers with special needs and aqua-mobility courses are run for those with muscle and ligament problems caused by such conditions as arthritis and osteoporosis.

There are other specialist sessions including parent and baby courses for those aged from six months to four-and-a-half years, where a parent or guardian accompanies the child. From three-and-a-half to school age, children can move on to the pre-school group. Juniors are from four-and-a-half up and these classes cover all aspects of water skills. The Star Award Scheme includes stroke techniques, distance, life saving and water safety, speed, stamina and poolside safety. There are also adult courses ranging from beginners to advanced levels. People come in from surrounding towns to make use of all the excellent facilities.

Golf

Golf is an extremely popular pastime throughout the country and Brentwood is fortunate to have a number of courses in and around the area. Many people travel in to play, often staying in local hotels. The clubs are also popular with golf societies.

Brentwood Golf Centre at Hartswood

This is a municipal golf course owned and operated by Brentwood Borough Council. It is situated off the Ingrave Road and is on part of King George's Playing Fields, approximately one mile south of the centre of the town. It is a mature parkland course with a length of 6,196yds and eighteen holes, and has been described as one of the finest municipal golf courses in the south-east of England.

Warley Park Golf Club

This popular and much sought-after club has a twenty-seven-hole course. It was first constructed as an eighteen-hole course in 1973. Within two years a further nine holes were added with the result that there can be various combinations of the courses. This is a club that is easily accessible from the M25, meaning that visitors can come from south of the Thames, from London or the Home Counties. The Lakes View restaurant offers meals from 7.30 a.m. This too is described as a mature parkland course.

Warley Park
golf course.

Weald Park Golf and Country Club

This is a fairly new club with its own interesting hotel in a courtyard setting. The outside of the
hotel has a traditional barnyard style, but inside there are all the necessary twenty-first-century
luxuries. La Chanterelle restaurant overlooks a small lake and the building is attractively
beamed. The club is in 150 acres of gentle rolling hills and is a very attractive place to both stay
and play.

The eighteen-hole golf course covers 6,386yds. It was constructed in 1992–93 and is
described as a par 71 championship golf course. There is a practice putting green, a short game
area and a 300yd practice range.

South Essex Golf Club

Situated in Herongate to the south of Brentwood, here the keen golfer will find twenty-seven
holes available on three nine-hole courses, called Heron, Hawk and Vixen. These provide great
variety as they can be played in any combination to make up a round of eighteen holes. South
Essex is on rising ground above the A127 to London and Southend, and there are fantastic
views to the south across the Thames and reaching as far as Kent.

This may be used as a 'pay and play' course and there is a fourteen-bay driving range, Crown
Golf Academy, a clubhouse, bar, restaurant and function room. 'Twilight Golf' is popular with
many players after a day at work. In spring, the bluebells are a delight to behold as you look
towards the trees.

Thorndon Park Golf Club

A great fire may have ravaged Thorndon Hall in 1878, but in 1920 a group of businessmen saw the potential of using part of the grounds as a golf course. They were offered a lease and appointed Harry Colt to design the course. In 1921, the east wing of the hall was leased as a clubhouse. A new clubhouse was built in 1974 when Thorndon Hall was sold and the interior restored and developed into luxury apartments.

Thorndon Hall Park makes a magnificent setting for the golf course and the fairways wind through ancient woodland dating back to the thirteenth century. This is a 6,512yd course, just two miles from the M25.

Bentley Golf Club

This club was established in 1972 and designed by Alec Swan of Golf Landscapes. Everything changed in 2004 when members purchased the club. A number of county events have been hosted by Bentley, including the Essex County Championships, the Essex Ladies County Championships and the Essex Foursomes. There are attractive water features on the 6,703yd course, which has eighteen holes. Facilities include a professional's shop, a practice ground and a clubhouse. This includes a licensed bar, a lounge and dining room and a separate spike bar.

Thorndon Hall, now converted into exclusive apartments.

Brentwood and District Historical Society

In Brentwood there are many people who take a keen interest in the history of the town, so it is no surprise to find that there is a thriving historical society. This originally came into being in the summer of 1941 following a public meeting. The aims of the group were 'to stimulate an interest in the history of the area, to collect information concerning the locality and to arrange lectures and excursions from time to time'. The original annual subscription was just 2s 6d.

Over the years the society has flourished and the membership has now grown to approximately 100. The programme is still based on lectures and excursions. Meetings are held at Brentwood County High School, as they have been since 1943. Most of the lectures concern Essex history and archaeology, with keen interest shown in local topics. In the early days, during the Second World War, many of the excursions were made by bicycle but times have changed and now coaches and private cars are the favoured mode of transport.

The Old County Ground

Merrymeade is a beautiful mansion which was once owned by Mr Robert Montgomery Horne-Payne. He was an executive of the Canadian Pacific Railway Co. and both he and his wife had a passion for cricket. Part of their estate became the County Cricket Ground and in the late nineteenth century the cricket club was founded. The house overlooked the pitch and the owners used to watch matches seated in the shade of a giant oak tree. The 1969 *Wisden Cricketers Almanac* stated that playing at Brentwood was like playing in the grounds of a country mansion.

Merrymeade, overlooking the Old County Ground.

The cricket club flourished and continues to do so. In recent years it has been awarded the Jack Pletchey Foundation Silver Achievement Award. Situated in Shenfield Road, it is within easy walking distance of the High Street. Tennis is also played on the site, with Brentwood Tennis Club originally being formed as a sub-section of the cricket club. At first the tennis club had just three courts available for use, but in 1904 the number increased to four and by the outbreak of the First World War, five were in use. During the war the club appears to have been in limbo, but afterwards it revived and in 1933 a pavilion was erected. Now there are eight synthetic courts and excellent floodlighting on six courts, making evening matches a possibility.

Hockey has also been played at the Old County Ground since 1902. Today there are seven mens teams and five ladies teams playing in leagues. There is also mixed hockey and great encouragement is given to young players, with junior teams ranging in age from eight to eighteen.

In 2003 the opportunity arose for members of the three clubs using the ground to purchase the freehold. This was a proud moment in the history of the Old County Ground. Those early players would find it difficult to recognise the ground now, especially those who played tennis.

The Essex Dog Training Centre

Dog walking is a popular and healthy pastime, yet a day can be ruined by an encounter with a rogue animal. With the superb Essex Dog Training Centre in Brentwood, there should be no excuse for such problems in the town.

This is a unique and very active group. Started by Roy Dyer more than thirty years ago, it has grown and flourished ever since. Roy has boundless enthusiasm and he has built the centre in Doddinghurst Road into what is probably the premier one of its kind in Europe. The nineteen instructors are all volunteers, but before they can start work they undergo a ten-week training course, a three-hour written examination and a two-hour practical test. This is a commitment to be taken very seriously.

There are classes for obedience, agility and puppy training, and the main aim is to build up trust between the dog and its owner. It is important that they each know what is expected of the other. Training is based on rewards, never on total domination, with treats for success and verbal praise being of primary importance.

When a new dog enters a home, the owners want it to become a part of the family. Early training is vital so the animal knows what is expected and the owner learns how to communicate. Puppy training classes are always popular and there are also obedience and agility courses held on Sunday mornings and Tuesday and Thursday evenings throughout the year, usually outside, but there are also excellent indoor facilities.

Roy is justly proud of his cynophobia classes. These are for those with a fear of dogs and the Brentwood Training Centre is the only venue in the county where this service is offered. Although mainly for children, adults too find these courses extremely helpful. Dogs with behavioural problems are also offered help and guidance.

The Essex Dog Display Team has built up a reputation not just locally, but nationally and internationally as well. It is the only civilian dog display team ever to be invited to appear at the Royal Tournament. This led to the team appearing before a live audience of over

Roy Dyer (far right) and members of the 'puppy training' class.

200,000 people, plus a huge television audience, as well as Her Majesty the Queen and many members of the royal family, all well-known dog lovers. Roy Dyer has made more than 100 television appearances, including visits to *Blue Peter* and *Dragons' Den*. He has also received an International Lifetime Achievement Award for his contribution to the canine world.

Brentwood Library

For many people, reading is an important interest and hobby. In the town there are two large book shops and also an excellent library. However, the building now used to house the library was not the original one in the town.

On the corner of Coptfield Road and Library Hill, a day nursery is to be found. This building was erected in 1851 to serve as the town's police station. It had outbuildings for cells, stables and a terrace of houses nearby for policemen and their families. It was no longer needed by the force when a purpose-built police station was opened at La Plata in 1937. At this time, the old building was taken over by the library service and it continued to be used for this purpose until 1987.

The new library stands in New Road facing the old courthouse, now used as a clinic. It is spacious and purpose-built and hosts many events throughout the year. It was not until 1991 that Princess Anne, the Princess Royal, visited the town and performed the official opening ceremony. A plaque commemorates this event.

Brentwood Writers' Circle

The town has a flourishing group of writers. Brentwood Writers' Circle was formed in 1941 when the founder, local author Elizabeth Baxter, could no longer travel to the London Writers' Circle. The first members met in her house in Park Road. Since those days there have been many changes, but the group has continued to meet monthly throughout the years. For a time Old House was used for meetings, but in recent years Fairview at the Ursuline Convent School has been the venue.

There are now sixty members and a waiting list of others keen to join. Interests vary and membership includes writers in many genres. Those interested in the written word, whether published or not, can join at any stage in their careers and are welcomed at meetings. Many members have now been published and those with successes include Elizabeth Lord, a prolific writer of historical romance, and Sylvia Kent, a freelance journalist and local historian. A number of members have also been commissioned to write local history books and there are published children's authors, short story writers, a lyricist and other freelance journalists.

The Bardswell Social Club

The club is situated close to the corner of Bardeswell Close and Weald Road and was founded in 1927. This was when a small band of railway trade unionists conceived the idea that there should be a meeting place for both business and recreation in Brentwood. At first meetings were held over a butcher's shop in the High Street before a piece of agricultural land was acquired complete with two cottages named 'Bardswell'. Originally all the land that now forms Bardeswell Close belonged to the club.

'Meet the Author' at Brentwood Library. From left to right: Sylvia Kent, Samantha Pearce, John Cassidy, Elizabeth Lord, James Shrubb (town crier), David Clark, Frances Clamp, Jim Reeve, Ted Bailey, Patricia Pound and John Roberts.

Frank King at the Bardswell Social Club.

At first the club was called the Brentwood and District TU and Labour Club and Institute Limited, and was registered on 15 June 1927. A sum of £1,200 was borrowed on simple interest terms at 6 per cent. By 1947, £1,200 in interest had been paid but the principal of £1,200 was still owed. A band of helpers came forward and a men's bar and small hall with two adjoining meeting rooms were erected. In 1948, with the assistance of the London Co-operative Society, the loan was redeemed and a reducing mortgage taken up for £1,000 repayable over ten years at 4 per cent. In fact, the debt was cleared in around eight-and-a-half years. At one time there was a bowling green, and snooker and darts were also played. It was very much a men's club and ladies had a separate room. Times have changed and now there is even a lady secretary.

In the following years there were various problems and the club almost folded in the mid-1950s. The land behind the building had been used for allotments and this area was put up for sale and finally sold for £2,500. This enabled debts to be cleared and some repairs to be undertaken. The land was used for the building of the houses in Bardeswell Close. Later, land that had been the club's bowling green was also sold, raising the sum of £2,400 and flats were erected.

In 1956 it was decided to change the name and the Bardswell Social Club was born. Beer was sold in those days at 1d below public house prices and a half-year's takings often amounted to £1,000 or less. The unpaid services of the committee and members were needed to ensure survival. Matters improved from 1965, but there is little doubt that the sale of land helped to keep the club afloat through the difficult years. (This information was supplied by Mr Frank King, who has been a keen club member since 1953 and a committee member for most of the years since then.)

Now various clubs use the facilities, including those for soul music, chess and Dungeons & Dragons. It is also used as a polling station and has become a venue for wedding receptions. The club is now flourishing once more, with a warm, friendly atmosphere. Since those early days in 1927 it has grown and changed, but the earlier spirit of the founders remains.

Dungeons & Dragons

The club started around twenty-eight years ago. Members have played at a number of different locations before settling at the Bardswell Social Club, where they now meet on Thursday evenings. There are various games played in the 'role play' format, with Dungeons & Dragons being the best known. This game was first seen in Great Britain in the film *ET*, but it was available before that. Now there are usually four games played on a Thursday night. The games concern individual struggles between good and evil. The plot often develops as the players talk while sitting around a table, but this is not always the case. A square board and small models of characters may be used. It is very much of a social activity where members meet with friends in a comfortable environment, unlike computer games which are usually played alone or with just one opponent.

Brentwood Chess Club

This club was first formed in 1932 when it was known as the Brentwood and Doddinghurst Chess Club. At first, meetings were held in Doddinghurst Church Manse, possibly because the rector was a keen chess player. There were just ten players in the embryonic Essex Chess League. During the years of the Second World War the club suspended its activities, but quickly resumed again in 1946.

Dungeons & Dragons players.

Since those early days meetings have been held at a number of different venues, but members have now settled happily at the Bardswell Social Club. Membership stands at over thirty with a very wide age range, the youngest being just nine years old. The club plays in a number of competitions. In fact, they field six teams, with four in the North Essex League and two in the Essex League. Brentwood Chess Club is now thriving and the future seems extremely bright.

Phoenix FM

In 1996, The Phoenix was formed to bring a new community based local radio service to Brentwood, Billericay and the surrounding area. At first the station could only make brief broadcasts, but for ten years those involved with the station lobbied the Radio Authority and later Ofcom to be granted a permanent broadcasting licence. Altogether there were twelve short-term broadcasts.

In April 1998 the name of the station changed from The Phoenix to Phoenix FM. Early on the recording studio was very small, being behind the Council's Tourist Information Office in Ongar Road. Later there was a move to the Hermitage Arts Centre in Shenfield Road, before another move, in 2001, to Hutton Poplars Lodge in Shenfield. The station is justifiably proud of the fact that they were the first community station to stream programmes on the internet.

February 2006 was a momentous time for the station when Ofcom confirmed that Phoenix FM had been awarded a permanent licence. Full-time programmes started in March 2007 at the brand new studios in Brentwood's Baytree Centre.

Phoenix FM is now a very active radio station. There are interviews with local people and plenty of music to cover a wide range of tastes. News reports can be heard and information is given concerning local activities and events in the area. This is a great service for the community with, via the internet, a very wide audience, keeping those who have moved away in touch with their former home.

Michelle Ward at work at Phoenix FM.

9

A Year in the Life of Brentwood

We have already seen that Brentwood has always been a town of passage. Even before there was any real settlement the Romans must have passed over the land where the town now stands as they travelled from London and the towns to the east. In the Middle Ages pilgrims paused briefly on their way to Canterbury. Later, horse-drawn coaches were pulled up the Brook Street hill and passengers would have used the many inns to be found in the town for refreshment, much as we now use service stations on major roads. Soldiers spent time at the Warley Barracks before being sent on to other destinations. The railway came and passengers probably noticed the name without necessarily knowing anything about the town. More recently the M25 has been built and it passes to the west of Brentwood. Junction 28 is frequently mentioned on traffic bulletins, but the majority of vehicles speed by on their way to other destinations.

This might give the impression that Brentwood is a quiet town with little happening. However, that is very far from the truth. Nearly 200 different clubs and associations are listed in *Network*, a local information magazine covering the whole district. There are other clubs not listed, many of which are associated with churches. Activities cover a wide range of interests including drama, writing, a racing pigeon club, winemaking, musical groups and many more. Throughout the year, there are also special events. In the following pages it will only be possible to look at a few of these, and we will consider just one year, 2009. Some of the events included occur annually, others will happen just once.

January

After all the activity and excitement of December and Christmas, January is often a quiet month. However, this is the time when many shops start their sales and the High Street and surrounding shopping streets become busy with eager bargain hunters.

It is also the time when many organizations restart after a short break, and this is certainly the case in the town. Brentwood Town Football Club, playing in the Ryman League, restarts playing matches both at home and away. The home ground is The Arena, next to the Brentwood Centre.

January sales start in Brentwood High Street.

Each year *The Yellow Advertiser*, one of the town's local newspapers, runs a ghost story competition. Members of Brentwood Writers' Circle are always encouraged to enter and, over the years, the group has had a number of winners. Yet everyone who has contributed to the competition has a chance to share their efforts with the other members. This happens at the first meeting in January. Candles are lit, spine-chillers read and afterwards mince pies, contributed by the committee, are enjoyed by all.

February

The weather is usually cold and rather depressing in February, but the town always has a busy social diary. In fact, *Network* lists forty-eight separate events during the month, some of which run over several days.

The Toy Collectors' Fair attracts plenty of interest and is held at the Brentwood Centre. Organised by John and Julie Webb, with their son David working as the show manager, contributors come from throughout the country and usually around 250 tables are taken. Although many of the exhibitors are shopkeepers, there are also some private sellers who enjoy the busy atmosphere. The Toy Fair comes to town approximately every two months, but February is the first visit when the toys brighten the dull days of winter.

A very popular musical group is the Brentwood Philharmonic Orchestra. Although they give four concerts each year, the first is usually in February. There are approximately sixty very enthusiastic musicians who most frequently perform at the Brentwood Ursuline School. This is also where rehearsals take place, although occasionally the hall at Bishops Hill or the Brentwood Cathedral are used for performances. Originally the group played at Fairkytes in Hornchurch and later in Upminster, but for around twenty-five years Brentwood has been their home. At the moment the main conductors are Alan Pegrum and Roger Lawrence. Brentwood Philharmonic Orchestra is supported by the Brentwood Arts Council.

Also in February, many of the area's runners take to the roads or the parks for early races. One such group is the Billericay Striders. They organise an event in Weald Park which is very well supported by other local teams, and keen followers prepare welcome refreshments for the exhausted competitors at the end of the morning.

March

As the weather improves, both indoor and outdoor events start to take place. An annual charity event is the Brentwood Half Marathon and Fun Run which occurs in March. Many of the more serious competitors use this as preparation for the later London Marathon. There is a real party atmosphere before the start of the race and in 2009, more than 3,500 competitors gathered at the start. Around 2,000 onlookers cheered the athletes on their way, balloons were held aloft and the junior band of the Royal British Legion played rousing music. The winner came home in just under one hour and ten minutes.

Setting off shortly after the half-marathon competitors are the fun runners. This too is a very popular annual event and many of those taking part don fancy dress as they set off to cover the three-mile course. At the time of writing, the half marathon has been held for twenty-eight years, ever growing in popularity and now welcoming runners from throughout Essex.

Runners in Weald Park.

Above left: Marshalls ready for the start of the half marathon.

Above right: The Brentwood Half Marathon.

March is when the Essex Book Festival takes place. This event started in 1999 and attracts well-known writers from Essex and beyond. Melvyn Bragg, Joan Bakewell, Roy Hattersley, Barbara Erskine and many more have been included in the programme. Brentwood has always supported the festival with venues being made available and local writers, bookshops and the library each making their own contribution.

This is also the month when two lucky eleven-year-olds are chosen from local primary schools to shadow the Mayor for a day. Needless to say, this is a great experience for the fortunate youngsters.

April

Easter, being a moveable feast, sometimes falls in March and at other times in April. In 2009, it fell in April. One important event on Good Friday is the annual 'Walk of Witness' from St Thomas' Church to the chapel ruins where the pilgrims travelling to Canterbury once worshipped. This is an inter-denominational event when several hundred members from many local churches join together to follow three men carrying a large wooden cross. They usually walk from the church, along the High Street before finally reaching the ruins of the chapel for a service. One feels that those pilgrims from the past would have approved of this act by people in the twenty-first century.

Another local group that has flourished for the past twenty years is the Brentwood Video Club. From small beginnings, following a course at the Bishops Hill Adult Education Centre, the membership has grown to around twenty-five and meetings are now held each Thursday evening for thirty-eight weeks of the year at St Thomas' Church Hall. This is a mixed group where all enthusiasts are welcomed.

The main aim of the club is to help and encourage members to make video films, and that includes advice on trimming clips, adding music, titles and voiceovers and other ways to make lively and interesting films. A film show takes place in February when the results of the year's efforts are shown and discussed. April is an important month for the club as it is when the annual dinner is held. This is a much-enjoyed event when partners are also welcomed to join the festivities.

May

Brentwood Library stands in New Road and was built in 1987. Some refurbishment took place in 2009 giving the building a spacious feel with a large area available for special events. The library is very active with a busy programme, especially during May. In this month in 2009, there was an 'Adult Learners Week', which began with a 'Living Library Day'. A number of local enthusiasts from many different fields came along to talk to members of the public about their speciality. At the pilot meeting, these included a professional photographer talking about his work in the 1960s, a human rights lawyer, an interior designer, a war veteran and many more. Similar events are planned for the future. Each month there are three 'Audio Reading Groups'; the Essex Blind Charity, Age Concern and Stroke Awareness. There has been a visit from Hutton Mothers' Union and a tea party for volunteers from the Home Libraries Services. A regular 'Baby and Toddler Rhyme Time' also takes place weekly. The month ended with an 'Egyptian Morning', which was enjoyed by the children and included a treasure hunt and a very colourful belly dancing display.

This is the month too when a new Mayor is appointed. In Chapter 7, Councillor Dudley Payne recalled special events from his year of office. He also mentioned the charities he had supported. At the end of his year in office, he was delighted to present £6,000 to the Claire-Louise Ferris Memorial Fund and £5,700 to the Ingrave Community Centre.

Above left: The Good Friday 'Walk of Witness'.

Above right: The 'Egyptian Morning' at the library.

June

This is the month of the Weald Show, and what an impressive event it is. For two days the Medieval Siege Society set up a tented village in Weald Park with many members in authentic dress only too willing to stop, chat and explain their skills. Costumed archers are able to demonstrate how bows and arrows were used.

During the two days it was also possible to watch mock tournaments and battles, as well as to enjoy other displays and exhibitions including dogs, lumberjacks, cheerleaders and a classic car parade. This is a family fun time that can be enjoyed by everyone.

Every year Brentwood welcomes cyclists from children to world-class riders in the adult section. This is for the Brentwood Town Centre Cycle Races. The High Street, Hart Street and part of Crown Street are all closed from 6 a.m. to 8 p.m. so that the competitors can compete in safety.

Under-8s take part in a 5km race, under-10s manage 9km with under-12s competing over 15km. The under-14s race over 20km and those under-16 undertake 25km. The adult men's circuit covers 38km and here competition is fierce for the cash prizes. This is a day when there are also other entertainments for those who come along to enjoy the fun. Sadly, in 2009, the race was unable to be run as the High Street was involved in major road work. As cobble stones are included in the new High Street road surface, there is some doubt that the race will again be run at this venue.

June is also the month when strawberries are at their best and Brentwood celebrates with its own Strawberry Fair. This is held on Shenfield Common and is a very popular event. There are craft stalls, entertainments for children, a parade of classic cars and, above all, plenty of beautiful ripe strawberries!

July

In July many clubs, schools and other organizations have end of session celebrations before the break for the summer holidays. Barbecues are popular too and historic Thorndon Park South is very well used in the area where this is permitted, especially on Sundays.

For nearly twenty-seven years Camp Beaumont has been running adventure day camps at Brentwood School, starting in July and continuing into August. The activities are many and varied and children are divided into a wide range of age groups, from nursery age to teenagers. The swimming pool is always a popular favourite and the sixty acres of playing fields mean that there is plenty of scope for outdoor pursuits when the weather is fine. There is an indoor sports hall, an arts and crafts studio and the chance to learn archery.

This is also the month of the very popular Brentwood in Bloom competition. There are many categories, each one sponsored by a different local firm or organization. These include an ever-popular schools project, the best front garden, the best team effort, the best-kept public house, the best business premises, the best maintained allotment, the best maintained religious grounds, the best environmental entry and the best residential accommodation garden. It is always pleasing to see those in retirement homes working together in the communal gardens. The Brentwood in Bloom group was founded in 1999 and has flourished ever since.

Above left: A medieval village is set up in Weald Park, complete with archers.

Above right: The garden around St George's Church is often a winner in the Brentwood in Bloom competition.

August

In August many people go away on their summer holidays. Nevertheless, a number of activities continue in the town. There is the Guild of Essex Craftsmen's Working Art and Craft Show at Ingatestone Hall. Guild artists are able to show and demonstrate their work. Shenfield Floral Art Club also has an evening when the skills of flower arranging are demonstrated to members and friends. The Ingatestone Garden Centre is busy with various demonstrations. This is a beautiful setting as the centre is a real horticulturalist's dream, with many unusual plants available to purchase. Both children and adults are catered for at various events.

Brentwood Library hosts the 'Summer Reading Challenge' throughout the school holidays, as do other local libraries. Children are encouraged to read six books to get a medal and older groups are asked to complete six quests. Even if participants are too young to read for themselves, they can still join in as someone older can read to them. For those over the age of ten there is a separate activity and children can join in at any time. Prizes can be won when all the challenges have been completed.

September

As the children return to school, we often enjoy a spell of good weather. Many clubs and organizations restart after the long August break and this is certainly true in Brentwood. The diary of events for the month to be found in *Network* records over fifty functions and there are many more that are not reported.

The Wedding Show has been taking place at the Brentwood Centre for eleven years. This is organised by the Wedding Event Company. A marquee is set up behind the centre and prospective brides, grooms, their families and all those involved in planning weddings are able to come along and discover what is available for that very special day. From the moment they arrive, visitors are made to feel important. Wine and canapés are available. There are goody bags for the brides, fashion viewings every hour, spot prizes and treats.

Above left: Celia Reed, an expert spinner, is a keen member of the Guild of Essex Craftsmen.

Above right: The World's Biggest Coffee Morning. Participants enjoy good company and raise money for charity at St Andrew's Church.

Many firms exhibit their wares, including bridal gowns, cakes, stationery and even the transport to take the parties to the wedding venue. This may be a stretch limo, an antique car or even a horse and carriage. During the two days that this event is held, several thousand interested prospective customers are expected to arrive.

Workshops and exhibitions are always popular. Ingatestone Hall has various displays, which in 2009 included one of historic clothes from medieval times to the 1940s. Ingatestone Garden Centre is a popular venue for workshops, especially with members of the Guild of Essex Craftsmen. Recently they have held a working art show and a September demonstration of spinning by Celia Reed. 2009 is the twenty-fifth anniversary of the guild, which attracts talented members from throughout Essex.

Celia Reed comes from Ingatestone and has enjoyed the craft of spinning for twenty-six years. In her talks and demonstrations she follows the story of spinning from ancient times to the present day. She originally became enthusiastic about her subject when she joined an activity holiday on a farm. There she first tried using an old-fashioned spinning wheel found in a cow shed! Today she travels with a portable Ashford spinning wheel which incorporates the ideas used in the old wheels, but using modern technology. Among other things, Celia makes and sells hand-spun wool, sheep-themed cards and handmade bookmarks.

Throughout the year there are musical concerts at St Thomas' Church. A number of these take place at lunchtime and September saw an unusual trombone octet playing to an enthusiastic audience. It was directed by Brian Lynn, who studied at the Guildhall School of Music and, like the other members of the octet, is a professional trombonist. He is also a keen member of the church choir and director of the orchestra of St Thomas'.

On the last Friday in September each year, the 'World's Biggest Coffee Morning' takes place. Throughout the country, coffee mornings are held in aid of the Macmillan Cancer Support Group. A number of these are enjoyed in Brentwood and one was at St Andrew's Church, Herongate. It was certainly a very friendly occasion. Organised by Mrs Julie Cristin, donated cakes and coffee were enjoyed in the church hall. Many of those who were unable to attend, but who have heard about the event, sent in a financial contribution to this very worthwhile fund.

October

As the ground becomes covered in fallen leaves and trees begin to lose the green of summer and take on the golden hues of autumn, indoor activities become increasingly popular. There are various concerts and in October 2009, Billericay Operatic Society took over Brentwood Theatre to put on a lively show which included songs from *Godspell* and dramatised versions of several parables.

Ropers Yard, off Hart Street, has a number of small boutique-type shops and one of these opened in October. This is Image Flooring Depot. This Essex-based company first started in Benfleet ten years ago and now has a number of stores across the county, but this is the first to adopt a boutique image. Claire Bell recalls how she first saw the little shop and fell in love with the building.

> We know everything about our product. As a town has a history, so does every piece of wood in the shop and each one has its own story. To take just one product: it is European oak that has been air dried for thirty-six months and then kiln dried between seven and fourteen weeks. This means that it becomes extremely stable. It is unique to get such long and wide boards and the wood can be treated in many different ways. Hand nails can be put in, or it can be sculptured or aged.

This is a unique outlet with experts who really know their product, and individual service can be given to each customer.

In October Brentwood Library welcomed Anita Marie Sackett, a poet who spent five years living and working in the Caribbean. This experience has had a great influence on her work. During her Saturday morning in the library, her audience of both children and adults heard stories and poems with a Caribbean flavour.

Anita was based in Kingston, Jamaica, and during her time there in the 1970s she collected many artefacts which now enhance her talks. These include coral, sea fern and shells, but they can be used to explain to children why they should no longer be collected. This event was part of the Essex Poetry Festival and was obviously enjoyed by all those present. Anita is a member of Brentwood Writers' Circle and is the Poetry Representative of the Society of Women Writers & Journalists.

At the end of the month, Halloween is celebrated with many shops making impressive window displays and some of the staff joining in with the spirit of the day by dressing up in suitable costumes. Children and parents enthusiastically clustered around Ali Cardabra as he performed magic tricks in the Baytree Centre.

Above left: Claire Bell of the Image Flooring Depot in Ropers Yard.

Above right: Anita Marie Sackett at the library for a Caribbean morning.

November

As the colours of autumn begin to fade, shops start arranging their Christmas displays. The end November 2009 also saw the re-opening of the High Street to traffic. At first this was a slow start, with lights controlling progress as the contractors continued putting the finishing touches to their work.

From the very start of the month bonfire parties were held and each evening the smell of smoke filled the air as fireworks rose skywards. A new company ran the fireworks display at the Brentwood Centre and there was the usual gathering at Button Common to celebrate Bonfire Night.

War memorials throughout the borough saw unusually large crowds gathering. Led by the Royal British Legion Youth Band, members of the town's uniformed organizations joined veterans from the Second World War to march from the Town Hall, along Middleton Hall Lane to the War Memorial. The 'Last Post' sounded, flags were dipped and two minutes of silence began. Later many wreaths were laid in memory of all those who have fallen in wars both past and present. Fianlly the parade marched to St Thomas' Church, where a service was held.

'Meet the Author' is an occasional event held at Brentwood Library. November saw twelve local authors display their books and a keen group of interested readers soon gathered. Some budding writers came for advice and, with a wide range of genres covered, there was something for everyone.

The High Street was finished and ready for re-opening, but first it was completely closed to traffic on the last afternoon of the month. This was the day when the Christmas lights were switched on by the Mayor, Councillor Tony Sleep. Children enjoyed fairground rides, while there were also street entertainers, food stalls and a Continental market outside the Baytree Centre. Thousands came to join in and shops that had been badly hit during the road works were able to enjoy good custom.

Above left: The Fruit 'n'Veg Shop in the High Street with a fine Christmas display.

Above right: The Royal British Legion Youth Band lead the procession on Remembrance Sunday.

December

There is always a feeling of excitement in the air as Christmas approaches. Shop windows prepare inviting displays and carols can be heard as you pass through the doors. For High Street traders in Brentwood, November was a difficult month, with the road closed to traffic for much of the time. However, as the new month dawned, with vehicles flowing once more, there was an increased feeling of optimism.

Christmas bazaars are always popular and schools and churches often take this opportunity to raise extra funds. Ingrave Johnstone Church of England Primary School was one of these and they were delighted to welcome Father Christmas to his grotto on the first Saturday in the month. He also visited Hutton All Saints Church of England Primary School later in the month. The United Reform Church in New Road was also the scene of a Christmas bazaar, with profits going to St Raphael's Club for the Disabled.

Carol concerts are very much a part of the festive season as well. Brentwood Choral Society performed in St Thomas' Church, assisted by the choir of St Thomas' School.

Christmas music was enjoyed by the Brentwood Townwomen's Guild and there was a concert in Brentwood Cathedral by the cathedral singers and choirs, joined by the Brentwood Choral Society. Ingatestone Choral Society also performed at the United Reform Church in Ingatestone.

This is also an important time of year for the Jewish community, with a party to celebrate the last day of Hanukkah, the lighting of the nine-branched menorah and presents for the children.

The town had a large Christmas tree decorated with blue lights close to the chapel ruins and all the local churches will have special services to celebrate the Christmas festival.

10

Towards the Future

In May 2009, part of the High Street closed ready for a multi-million pound improvement scheme and the work was finally completed at the end of November. There is little doubt that the centre of the town will be dramatically changed by the time all the plans for the future of Brentwood are in place.

The chapel in the High Street has always played a very important role in the history of the town. From the days when the hamlet was first developing, it was needed for the use of the visiting pilgrims. In fact, the monks of St Osyth's Priory were allowed to clear forty acres of woodland in the parish of South Weald as early as 1177. This was where a settlement developed, along the main London to Colchester road. Here, in 1221, the chapel was built in the hope that it would be self-financing as travellers and pilgrims made donations on their way to Canterbury.

Since the partial demolition of the High Street chapel, the surrounding area has altered dramatically. A large retail development dominates the ruin and plants have been grown behind a low brick wall to the south, partly hiding the remains of the building. There are benches around the site, but these are turned away from the building.

In the planned development of the chapel area, it is hoped that this vital link in the history of the town will become a significant feature of the whole area.

The Premier Inn

For a number of years the tall tower of the Amstrad offices dominated the dip in Kings Road, close to the railway station. Then the building was taken over by the Premier Inn chain of hotels and complete refurbishment took place before it opened its doors to the public in October 2009.

This is an unusual development for the company as they do not normally use tower blocks, but the 122 rooms have been carefully designed to maintain the usual high standard of comfort and there is an excellent restaurant on the ground floor.

The arrival of the Premier Inn is an important development in the town. The old coaching inns and small hotels are still available for many, but the way in which people travel has changed over the years. Many visit the town for work and stay for perhaps one or two nights. Hotels close to the main transport links cater for these needs. The Holiday Inn is near to the M25 and a new hotel complex is planned for a site close to the Mountnessing Roundabout beside the busy A12.

Road refurbishment led to the High Street being closed for more than a month in 2009.

The Premier Inn arrives in Brentwood, taking over the refurbished Amstrad building. Here we see the Mayor at the official opening.

Looking Ahead
(Information supplied by a Planning Officer)

Each authority in England has to provide a local development plan. This is normally expected to cover a minimum of fifteen years and Brentwood is in the early stages of a new scheme to replace the current local plan, which was adopted in 2005. Consultations take place with all interested parties to decide what the town should be like in the future. Because this is ongoing, it is impossible to be specific at the moment. Probably it will be decided that what is best about Brentwood at the moment should be conserved, together with improvements for the quality of the life of residents. Outside elements, such as national or regional planning policy, will also influence what happens in the future.

The Town Hall, with the clock originally on the Victorian building in the High Street.

Brentwood is a town within the Metropolitan green belt and it has always been seen as an area of restraint. It is a high-quality town, surrounded by small, attractive villages in an appealing rural landscape. These are the sort of characteristics that the Council will almost certainly want to preserve after consultation with residents.

Because of the town's important green belt location, it is realised that we must not put too much pressure on this very precious region, but there may come a time when the town runs out of land in the existing urban areas. Equally, there is a concern that constant development in the town with high-density building will have an adverse impact on the character of the urban area.

In the future there will almost certainly be continued protection of the green belt, and of the character of the whole area and its surrounding villages. The enhancement of the High Street and the town centre will continue. The High Street improvement scheme, in partnership with Essex County Council, has now been completed. It is believed that this will provide significant environmental improvements for the public so that pedestrians will have an improved experience. The balance between pedestrians and traffic will be improved.

It is also hoped that Brentwood will retain its competitiveness as a shopping area. It will be impossible to compete with Lakeside or Bluewater, but Brentwood is different. It is a local convenience shopping centre and it is hoped that the town will offer a choice of shopping experience that larger centres cannot provide. Independent small traders in specialist shops will be encouraged alongside the larger chain stores. It is hoped that Brentwood will remain an attractive place for local shoppers and that the town centre will concentrate not only on being a shopping focus, but also on cultural, leisure and community activities. It is also an important place of employment.

Brentwood grew as a town along the old Roman road and it remains a town of passage. The Council is also looking to enhance the leisure attractions of the town and its tourism role by offering more hotel accommodation. As mentioned above, the Premier Inn has opened near the station and another new hotel is planned close to the Mountnessing Roundabout by the A12. However, Brentwood has its own unique character. It is not part of London and must remain outside. It is an Essex town that has grown up into what it is today: a small, attractive green belt town, and it is to be hoped that that is how it will remain. However, businesses must be persuaded to stay within the area and become ever more successful, thus helping the local economy.

This is a commuter town with excellent road and rail links. In the future it is hoped there will be a greater availability of jobs so that perhaps more people will have greater choice as to whether they live and work in Brentwood. At the moment, many residents with higher-value jobs commute out and others in the service sector travel in. The government wants to reduce the need to travel, particularly by car.

There is a Brentwood Renaissance Group for the town centre, building on the High Street improvements. It is a joint venture by Essex County Council and Brentwood Borough Council. There are also other partners involved, including the Chamber of Commerce. The aim is to take the town centre forward. The chapel ruins are already a focal point, but offer an opportunity to further improve the public domain.

William Hunter car park is a large site with the potential for improving the choice of shopping and other leisure activities. This is a rare opportunity, just behind the High Street, where there can be development without the need to demolish other properties. The new leader of the Council has identified the needs of the young and the elderly as issues she particularly wants to take forward in developing plans for the future.

When the Crossrail project is finished, travel from Shenfield to the west side of London should improve. The completion of the High Street improvement scheme allows for a greater choice of routes, taking some unnecessary traffic away from the High Street.

The High Street reopened to traffic after refurbishment. Various surfaces have been introduced, including cobbles to reduce speeds.

The fountains outside the Sainsbury's superstore.

Towards Tomorrow

Since the Middle Ages, when the small hamlet of Brentwood catered for the needs of pilgrims, there have been many changes and the town is now a thriving centre for trade and commerce. It is still a town of passage, but it is also a place where many come to settle and enjoy the variety of amenities offered. There are superb schools, good shops and activities to suit all tastes. The face of the town is changing, but it is to be hoped that the spirit which makes it such a pleasant place to live will continue to flourish in the future.

Bibliography

Acton, Doreen, *A History of Brentwood Baptist Church* (Brentwood Baptist Church)

Copeland, J., *Images of Brentwood* (Tempus Publishing)

Ellis, T. Jon, *Bishops Hall & Estate* (published privately)

Fryer, John, *Brentwood: A Pictorial History* (Brentwood Town Centre Partnership)

Fryer, John, and Perrior, Geoffrey, *Brentwood in Old Postcards Volume 3* (European Library)

Hewson, Don, *Brentwood, Shenfield & Warley* (Sutton Publishing)

Hough, John, *Essex Churches* (The Boydell Press)

Kent, Sylvia, *Brentwood: A Photographic History* (Black Horse Books)

Larkin, John, *Fireside Talks about Brentwood* (Sharon Publications)

le Lievre, Audrey, *Miss Willmott of Warley Place* (Faber Finds)

Lloyd, John, *The Place at Brook Street* (Marygreen Books)

Marriage, John, *Bygone Brentwood* (Phillimore & Co. Ltd)

Simpson, Frank, *Brentwood in Old Postcards* (European Library)

Simpson, Frank, *Brentwood in Old Postcards Volume 2* (European Library)

Tames, Richard, *Brentwood Past* (Historical Publications Ltd)

Ward, Jennifer, *Brentwood: A History* (Phillimore & Co. Ltd)

Various guidebooks

Other titles published by The History Press

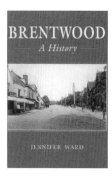

Brentwood: A History
JENNIFER WARD

Brentwood began as a small settlement in a woodland clearing on the London to Colchester road over 800 years ago. Gradually it developed into a small market town where medieval pilgrims stopped on their way to the shrine of St Thomas à Becket at Canterbury. Now a busy commuter town, it has grown rapidly since 1945. Readable and entertaining, this book is also lavishly illustrated and will appeal to a wide readership.

978 1 8607 7279 5

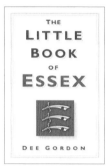

The Little Book of Essex
DEE GORDON

The Little Book of Essex is packed full of entertaining bite-sized pieces of historic and contemporary trivia that come together to make essential reading for visitors and locals alike. It can be described as a compendium of frivolity, a reference book of little-known facts, or a wacky guide to one of England's most colourful counties. Be amused and amazed at the stories and history of Essex's landscape, towns, villages, heritage, buildings and, above all, its people.

978 0 7509 5127 2

Haunted Essex
CARMEL KING

From heart-stopping accounts of apparitions, manifestations and related supernatural phenomena, to first-hand encounters with phantoms and spirits, this collection of stories contains both new and well-known spooky tales from around the county of Essex. This phenomenal gathering of ghostly goings-on is bound to captivate anyone interested in the supernatural history of the area.

978 07524 5126 8

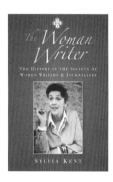

The Woman Writer: The History of the Society of Women Writers & Journalists
SYLVIA KENT

To celebrate the centenary of the birth of the SWWJ's much-loved President of twenty-two years, Joyce Grenfell, the Society's archivist, Sylvia Kent, reveals the long and fascinating history of the Society. Not only is it's evolution fully explored, but also the lives of many of its members have been thoroughly researched to paint a vivid picture of how it has gone from strength to strength.

978 0 7524 5159 6

Visit our website and discover thousands of other History Press books.

www.thehistorypress.co.uk

The History Press